Politics and Passion

Politics and Passion

Toward a More
Egalitarian Liberalism

MICHAEL WALZER

YALE UNIVERSITY PRESS   NEW HAVEN & LONDON

The appendix and earlier versions of five of the chapters were previously published and are reproduced by permission of the publisher.

"The Communitarian Critique of Liberalism," *Political Theory: An International Journal of Political Philosophy* 18, no. 1 (February 1990): 6–23. Reprinted by permission of Sage Publications, Inc.

"Deliberation, and What Else?" In Stephen Macedo, ed., *Deliberative Politics: Essays on Democracy and Disagreement* (New York: Oxford University Press, 1999), copyright © 1999 by Oxford University Press, Inc. Used by permission of Oxford University Press, Inc.

"Equality and Civil Society." In Simone Chambers and Will Kymlicka, eds., *Alternative Conceptions of Civil Society* (Princeton: Princeton University Press, 2002): 34–49. Reprinted with permission.

"On Involuntary Association." In Amy Gutmann, ed., *Freedom of Association* (Princeton: Princeton University Press, 1998): 64–74. Reprinted with permission.

"Passion and Politics," *Philosophy and Social Criticism* 28, no. 6 (2002): 617–633. Reprinted by permission of Sage Publications Ltd.

"What Rights for Illiberal Communities?" In Daniel A. Bell and Avner de-Shalit, eds., *Forms of Justice: Critical Perspectives on David Miller's Political Philosophy* (Lanham, Md.: Rowman and Littlefield Publishers, Inc., 2003): 123–134. Reprinted with permission.

Designed by James J. Johnson and set in Ehrhardt Roman type by Integrated Publishing Solutions, Grand Rapids, Michigan. Printed in the United States of America by Vail Ballou Press, Binghamton, New York.

Library of Congress Cataloging-in-Publication Data

Walzer, Michael.
Politics and passion : toward a more egalitarian liberalism / Michael Walzer.
    p. cm.
Includes bibliographical references and index.
ISBN 0-300-10328-X (hardcover)
1. Liberalism. 2. Equality. I. Title.
JC574.W393   2005
320.51'3—dc22

A catalogue record for this book is available from the British Library.

The paper in this book meets the guidelines for permanence and durability of the Committee on Production Guidelines for Book Longevity of the Council on Library Resources.

10 9 8 7 6 5 4 3 2 1

This book is for Joe, Katya, Stefan, and Jules

Contents

INTRODUCTION

Liberalism and Inequality

LTHOUGH THE *L* WORD — LIBERALISM — was, for a time, pure poison in American politics, it has long been the universal antidote of American political theory. Liberal democracy is the rule of the many without its dangers— with minorities protected and human rights guaranteed. Liberal religion is a faith free of dogma—and a church that acknowledges the legitimacy of other churches. Liberal nationalism is the very opposite of a parochial or chauvinist ideology. A liberal revolution is pure velvet; it never ends in a reign of terror. Liberal authoritarianism describes an undemocratic regime that opens limited room for political dissent and individual freedom (and probably gets support from the American government). The liberal left has surrendered the ideological certainties of Marxist orthodoxy. The liberal right is ready at last to tolerate the liberal left.

Liberalism itself is more than the sum of all these antidotes. Many of its critics find it insufficiently nourishing, but they are wrong. The history of liberal politics is complicated and conflictual, and the outcome of that history is a substantial and powerful doctrine. Nonetheless, some very important features of human life are left out of this doctrine; it needs to be made more complicated and more inclusive.

Some years ago, I wrote an essay called "The Communitarian Critique of Liberalism," in which I argued that communitarianism is best understood as a corrective to liberal theory and practice (rather than as a freestanding doctrine or substantive political program).[1] My original intention in this book was to flesh out that "correction" and to suggest some of the ways liberalism might better encompass an understanding of politics, sociology, and social psychology. That is still a significant part of my plan, and it has governed my choice of subject matter for the six chapters. In the first four, I want to look closely at what I take to be a central fact about our associational life: over much of its range, it isn't the work of that liberal hero, the autonomous individual, choosing his or her memberships, moving freely from group to group in civil society. Instead, most of us are born into or find ourselves in what may well be the most important groups to which we belong—the cultural and religious, the national and linguistic communities within which we cultivate not only identity but character and whose values we pass on to our children (without asking them).

Our membership in these communities is also likely to determine, or at least to influence strongly, our standing in the social hierarchy and our central or marginal location in social space. There is room to move around in liberal societies, more room perhaps than in any other social formation; still, the room is more limited, our movements are more predictable, the difficulties we encounter are more common to ourselves and our fellows, than liberal theorists have been ready to admit. In the fifth chapter, I will argue in related fashion that the deliberations of autonomous individuals make up only a small part of the story of democratic politics. I will then suggest that social conflict, which has been neglected by liberal theorists in recent years, is the larger part of the story, and I will provide an account (or at least a list) of the activities it requires. In the sixth chapter, I will consider the role of passion in our political life and my worry that liberal reasonableness, to which I remain committed, does not help us to understand the importance of that role or to shape and constrain the different ways the role is played.

That is, or was, my program, but in the course of writing the book, I found myself increasingly engrossed by another set of problems, which have more to do with social democracy than with communitarianism. Focusing on the exclusions of liberal theory—involuntary association, collective powerlessness, the problems posed by cultural marginality, the hierarchies of civil society, the politics of social conflict, and the force of passionate engagement—I came to see that their most important effect is to make the struggle against inequality more difficult than it should be. So I also want to argue that with regard to this struggle, liberalism in its standard contemporary versions is an inadequate theory and a disabled political practice. It is inadequate, first of all, because inequality lives within and among those involuntary associations whose importance is insufficiently acknowledged in liberal theory; and those same associations are the main protagonists of multicultural politics, which is one of the forms (though contestable and contested) of contemporary egalitarianism. Standard liberalism is inadequate also because liberal theorists, while they have sometimes challenged, have only recently begun to engage creatively with, the more problematic features of multiculturalism and of civil society generally.[2] And it is inadequate because in the thoughtful discussions that liberal theory favors under the name of "deliberation," the discussants rarely address successfully the actual experience of inequality or the fight against it, even when they reach egalitarian conclusions. Finally, liberalism is inadequate because the social structures and political orders that sustain inequality cannot be actively opposed without a passionate intensity that liberals do not (for good reasons) want to acknowledge or accommodate. Accommodation is especially difficult when passion is, as it commonly is, the product of our attachments and belongings.

The communitarian correction that was my first aim can serve to produce a liberalism that is, not more egalitarian than the existing standard liberalism, but more available for egalitarian appropriation and use. This corrected version is politically more engaged, sociologically more informed, and psychologically more open—and these are necessary features, or so I shall argue, of any doctrine capable of encompassing, explaining, and supporting democratic mobilization and solidarity. I start from the assumption, which I won't defend here, that we need a doctrine of that sort and that it had better be a liberal doctrine. The ultimate justification for an egalitarian or anti-hierarchical politics is the difference it makes in the everyday life of individual men and women.

This ultimate justification is not, however, a sufficient guide for political action. For the inequalities that need to be overcome or curtailed are not simply individual inequalities. They impact different groups differently. They divide society not only between rich and poor but also between black and white, Anglo and Hispanic, French and Arab, German and Turk, Hindu and Muslim. And the differences among groups make a political difference. The old idea of the old left—that once the revolution abolished the class hierarchy, there would be no more inequality—seems to be wrong. It has never been tested, of course, but one reason for that is the failure of class politics to challenge the deepest inequalities of contemporary societies.

Multiculturalism is an effort to address those inequalities. Sometimes it is tough-minded and realistic; sometimes it is a little crazed. In neither case, however, can it be blamed for the failures that make it necessary. Some old-left writers claim that any kind of culturalist politics shatters the solidarity that makes the welfare state possible, undermines the unity of the working class, replaces universal values with chauvinist passion, and tolerates or even fosters the inner oppressiveness of traditional cultures. The last of these charges is the one that worries me the most; I will come back to it several times. The others, I believe, have little empirical basis.[3] In any case, I mean to defend a hardheaded, indeed, a materialist version of multicultural politics — "meat-and-potatoes multiculturalism" — and I will try to show how this politics could serve the cause of both liberalism and equality.

My six chapters deal with domestic society, chiefly, though not only, in the United States. In the conclusion I will suggest that a pluralist and social democratic liberalism also has something to say about the inequalities of international society. The terrible poverty of so many people, in the third world especially, cannot be addressed without attending to the groups to which they belong. Poor people are individuals, certainly, and need to be treated as such; but they are also members, and if their membership is sometimes antithetical to their individuality, it is also sometimes its necessary partner.

My project in this book is more widely shared today than when I began writing. Spurred in part by Will Kymlicka's *Liberalism, Community, and Culture,* liberal political theorists, and lawyers, too, have taken a growing interest in groups of the sort that I am concerned with here. Spurred in part by feminist critics like Susan Moller Okin, they have begun to deal with the problem of inequality within these groups.[4] Indeed, gender inequalities are right now the subject of intense debate in all liberal societies.

Some of the new attention to membership and its complications, especially in the legal literature, is concrete and detailed in ways that I admire but cannot imitate.[5] Much of American political debate takes place in the courts — not always the best place, in my view, but the place where the nuts and bolts of membership and equality are most often addressed. I shall only occasionally get to nuts and bolts in this book. My hope, instead, is to point provocatively to the whole range of issues raised by the deficiencies of what I will be calling standard liberalism. What and who have been left out of the standard version still matters, still makes a difference in how we think about politics and society.

Politics and Passion

ONE

Involuntary Association

THE PEOPLE I KNOW ARE CONSTANTLY FORMING associations, and they greatly value the freedom to associate as they please, with all sorts of people, for all sorts of purposes. They are certainly right: freedom of association is a central value, a fundamental requirement, of liberal society and democratic politics. But it is a mistake to generalize this value and try to call into being, in theory or in practice, a world where all associations are voluntary, a social union composed entirely of freely constituted social unions. The ideal picture of autonomous individuals choosing their connections (and disconnections) without constraints of any sort is an example of bad utopianism. It has never made sense to sociologists, and it ought to inspire skepticism among political theorists and moral philosophers, too. No human society could survive without connections of a very different sort. But how can connections of a different sort be justified to men and women who claim to be free?

Doesn't freedom require the breaking of all those bonds that we have not chosen or do not right now choose for ourselves? Aren't involuntary associations, the sentiments they generate, and the values they inculcate, a threat to the very idea of a liberal society?

Particular associations can indeed be a threat, not because they are involuntary but because they are xenophobic, hierarchical, or totalitarian. It is not pure voluntarism that freedom requires but the possibility of opposition and escape.[1] The possibility: while opposition is usually a good thing, escape is not always or necessarily so. We need not always make it easy to walk away from involuntary associations. Many valuable memberships are not freely entered into; many binding obligations are not entirely the product of consent; many strong feelings, many useful ideas, come unchosen into our lives.

We can think of our lives, and of the various collective lives in which they are embedded, as "social constructions" that we, as individuals, have had a hand in making; we cannot plausibly think of them as wholly made by ourselves. We join groups, we form associations, we organize and we are organized, within a complex set of constraints. These take many different forms, some of which are both valuable and legitimate. Remember Rousseau's famous lines from the first chapter of the *Social Contract:* "Man is born free; and everywhere he is in chains. . . . How did this change come about? I do not know. What can make it legitimate? That question I think I can answer."[2] But the opening is wrong; we are not born free.

And because we are not born free, we are not born equal. This may be more obvious. Involuntary association is the most immediate cause of inequality, for it consigns each person to a particular place or set of places in the social system. If we think of the hierarchies of property and status as the basic structures of an inegalitarian society, then involuntary association is the way men and women are locked into their ranks and orders. The promise of liberal autonomy has always been that it will break the locks, enabling individuals to choose or at least to aim at the places they desire—and so create a society of free and mobile men and women who are also (more nearly) equal. This is a false or, better, a wildly exaggerated promise. We will succeed in challenging the social hierarchy only if we recognize and work on the realities of involuntary association. Denial is foolish, and abolition is impossible. Involuntary association is a permanent feature of social existence, and the people who fight for equality, like those who struggle to be free, are inevitably its creatures.

There are four kinds of involuntary constraints to consider here. All of them are established very early in our lives; they press us toward, even force us into, associations of a certain sort; and they limit our right and our ability to leave, although in a liberal society they cannot do away with these entirely. Sociologists have written about the first two, political theorists and moral philosophers about the last two. But it is useful, I think, to regard them as items on a single list.

The first constraint is familial and social. We are born members of a kin group, of a nation or country, and of a social class; and we are born male or female. These four attributes go a long way toward determining the people with whom we associate for the rest of our lives (even if we hate our relatives, think patriotism sentimental, and never attain class or gender consciousness). Most of us are also admitted early on to one or another religious membership, perhaps through infant baptism, circumcision, adolescent confirmation, or bar mitzvah. These are concrete, involuntary joinings from which rights and responsibilities follow—as the child will certainly be told. But parental instruction—like religious and political socialization outside the home and like the everyday experiences of class and gender—also works more indirectly by creating background conditions that support particular adult associations and not others. A great deal has been written in recent years about family failure, but in truth most parents are remarkably successful at producing children much like themselves. Sometimes, unhappily, that is the sign of their failure—as when poor parents are unable to boost their children into middle-class society. But most parents want offspring who don't land too far off, whom they can still recognize as their own, and mostly they produce children like that. They get a little help, of course, from their friends.

Young people can break loose, tear themselves free from family ties and social circumstances, live outside the conventions of a gendered society, but only at a cost that most of them don't want to bear. That's why parental connections are by far the best predictors of their children's connections, as political scientists discovered long ago with regard to party allegiance and voting behavior. Despite the value attached to "independence" in American political culture, for example, children are mostly ready to follow the parental lead; just as Democratic and Republican children are likely to have Democratic and Republican parents, so independent children are likely to have independent parents.[3] Religious choices are also, most often, indicated by parental affiliation. Those early rituals of adherence are remarkably effective; religious membership is typically an inheritance. Protestant practices like adult baptism and evangelical rebirth are meant to disrupt this pattern, and do to some extent, in ways historically helpful to the practice of voluntary association.[4] Still, it would be interesting to know what percentage of born-again Christians are the spiritual as well as the bodily offspring of their parents: born to be born again.

Most people join associations that confirm rather than challenge their identities, and their identities are, mostly, the gifts of their parents and their parents' friends. Again, individuals can break away, committing themselves to the difficult process of self-formation, like the biblical Abraham, who (according to postbiblical legend) broke his father's idols, or like John Bunyan's Christian pilgrim (in *The Pilgrim's Progress,* the classic text of English Protestantism), who ran away from his wife and children in pursuit of his own salvation, putting his fingers in his ears so he wouldn't hear their cries. Social change is unimaginable without people who break away, but if all people were like that, society itself would be unimaginable. Nor did Abraham encourage a similar rebelliousness in his beloved son, Isaac. Isaac, unlike his father, was born a member of Jehovah's party; he was perhaps less admirable for that, but infinitely more reliable. And Bunyan was compelled by his readers to bring the pilgrim's wife and children along (in a sequel to *Pilgrim's Progress*) on what was by then a stereotypical journey to join the community of saints.[5]

The one break with the parental world that most parents are inclined to encourage, at least in modern societies, is movement up the established hierarchies. Even so, most children are only modestly mobile (up or down); class standing, like political and religious allegiance, tends to endure across generations—even when the mass media disrupt the transmission of class culture. This is so in part because of the continued existence of external obstacles to social mobility that we might plausibly hope to abolish for the sake of equal opportunity. Although the structures of subordination commonly reproduce themselves, they can sometimes be challenged and transformed. But there are also internal obstacles to social mobility, which have to do with the reluctance of children to give up the solidarities of class and neighborhood. Hence the children's propensity to enact their associational life within a social world that is already their own.

Associations formed or joined against a background of this sort can still be described as voluntary, but we need to acknowledge how partial and incomplete the description is. It will look even more incomplete after we consider the next item on my list.

The second constraint on voluntary association is the cultural determination of available associational forms. Associates may choose one another, but they rarely have much to say about the structure and style of their association. Marriage is the obvious example: the match may be a true meeting of minds, but the meaning of the match is not determined by the minds that meet. Marriage is a cultural practice; its meaning and the responsibilities it entails are accepted by the partners as soon as they acknowledge one another as husband and wife. Their prenuptial agreements and contracts affect only the details of the arrangement. Similarly, men and women can form a club or league or union or party; they can gather together freely and write their own bylaws. Their association is likely, however, to be remarkably similar to that of their fellow citizens down the road or across town, and bylaws are commonly written to a standard form.[6]

Creative individuals in periods of cultural crisis and transformation do manage to design new associational forms, often after many false starts and failed attempts. The structural inequalities of the old forms can be and often are criticized and changed from within. But their overcoming takes a long time, and the critical vision that guides the effort is unlikely to be fully realized even at the end of that time. Change can move in the other direction, too: toward more rigid and orthodox versions of the cultural status quo. The norm, nonetheless, is continuity—imitation and reiteration—interrupted periodically by reforming efforts to return the various associations to their first principles. The principles themselves are objects of allegiance even before they are objects of choice.[7]

Similarly, associational competence is admired and mimicked rather than freely chosen. We don't usually decide to learn the social and political skills that make association possible. Like bylaws and principles, skill is a cultural gift—which means that some subset of parents and elders pass it on, often without specifically trying to. My first association was a group of eight-year-olds, the Four Friends Forever, which lasted about ten months and left me better prepared for the next one. In a culture that values association and the competence that makes it possible, breakup is more often an incitement than a disillusion.

There is, then, a radical givenness to our associational life. We meet for a purpose, discover a common interest, agree more or less on a line of argument, and form an organization. Our organization is very much like all the others, *and that's how we know what we are doing*. That's why our accomplishment registers with the already existing groups, who quickly figure out whether we are potential competitors or allies, or neither, our union a matter of indifference. We arouse conventional expectations, and these are our passport to civil society. If, on the contrary, we meet in secret, wear masks, communicate in code, acknowledge no public purpose, and generally behave in nonstandard ways, we arouse uneasiness and suspicion. Perhaps we are not an association at all but a cabal, a conspiracy, or worse.

Even radically new associational practices are likely to mimic old forms—the way gay unions mimic the modern nuclear family and aim at the same legal recognition. The established model is found to be eminently usable, so long as one of its conventionally gendered constraints is set aside—but how difficult that setting aside can be. In somewhat similar fashion, antiparliamentary social movements drift toward partylike organization; religious sects turn themselves into churches, claiming all the while that they are churches with a difference (which they sometimes are).

Imagine people coming together in wholly different, infinitely odd ways, in free-form associations, with no one sending out recognizable signals: the social world would be unbearable—with constant uneasiness, endless suspicion. Imagine every marriage designed in lawless freedom by the two partners, without a standard model, not for the ceremony that unites them (this much is fairly common in the United States today), not for their commitment to one another, not for the proposed living arrangements, not for their obligations to in-laws and children. The partners might well be free and equal, but they would hardly be "married." The point of marriage would be lost. We would have to devise some other practice to stabilize social expectations and individual responsibilities. Free choice can work only within the limits of cultural provision.

The third constraint on voluntary association is political. Birth and residence make us members of a political community. Membership has different meanings in different times and places, and for some individuals sometimes (colonists in a new country, for example), it can be a matter of deliberate choice. But that is not what it is for most people. The standard critique of liberal consent theory builds on this simple fact about political life: we are born citizens (unless we are very unlucky) and are rarely invited to agree to our citizenship. The standard response to this critique is to posit some sort of tacit consent—as I did when I wrote about citizenship and obligation more than twenty-five years ago.[8] There are good reasons for this response, but it doesn't touch the point relevant here: that the political community is in an important sense a union shop. If you are here, and if you stay here, you are caught up in a set of arrangements that you had no part in designing.

Real union shops work in the same way and seem to me similarly justified.[9] Self-government, whether it takes the form of political or industrial democracy, is possible only if all the residents/workers are also citizens. They can choose to vote or not, to join this or that party or movement, to form a caucus or oppositional faction, or to avoid political activity entirely. But if they are denied, or if they deny themselves, the right to do these things, then democracy is replaced by the rule of some people over others. It may be that anyway, much of the time, but the possibility of citizen activism—associational militancy, mass mobilization, radical insurgency, electoral overturn—at least imposes some restraint on the rulers, and citizens can keep that possibility alive without ever doing anything (although sometimes, surely, they ought to do something). In any case, there is one thing they can't do: they can't live or work someplace and refuse the rights of citizenship—and the burdens, too, such as taxes and union dues.[10]

Compulsory membership in the state or the workers' union opens the way for new sorts of choices and decisions, including the decision to become an engaged citizen or a union activist. Membership isn't a precondition of activism, since noncitizens and workers without unions can associate, and often have, to demand political enfranchisement or union recognition. Note, however, that militants don't win this battle if they win it only for themselves. Victory pulls in the passive others, and it provides them with new opportunities and responsibilities. They can now volunteer, if they choose to, for activities and organizations more locally effective than anything available to them before. A full-fledged democratic politics is only now possible, and what makes it possible is the coerced membership of all the workers/citizens.

The fourth constraint on association is moral, which some people will take to mean that it does not constrain at all. Violators are subject only to exhortation and reproach. Unless morality is a feature of socialization, or written into the cultural code, or legally enforced by state officials, it may seem to have no practical effect. But this is wrong. Morality is indeed implicated in the socialization process, the cultural code, and the legal order—but it is also experienced as something separate from all three. It is a constraint that individuals confront not only as creatures of society, culture, and politics but also as individuals trying to do the right thing. They hear an internal voice of constraint, telling them that they should do this or that, which they have not (so far) chosen to do and would rather not do. Most important for my purposes here, the voice tells them (they tell themselves) that they ought to join this association or participate in that social or political struggle—or they ought not to abandon this association or withdraw from that struggle.

Moral constraints are often constraints on exit and, most interestingly, on exit from involuntary associations. The classic example is Rousseau's account of the right of emigration. Citizens, he says, can leave at any time, except when the republic is in danger. In time of trouble they are bound to stay and help their fellow citizens (the same argument probably applies to the members of subordinated social classes and minority races and religions, but I will stick for now to the political example).[11] This bond doesn't derive from their previous political participation. Even if they have been unenthusiastic, even negligent citizens, never hurrying to public assemblies, never voting, they are still obligated. Rousseau's assertion is unqualified. It is also entirely plausible. I have perhaps benefited from the republic's better days, or from the activism of my fellows, or from the schooling the republic provides, or from the good name of citizen, or simply from having had a secure place in the world. Now I must not walk away. Indeed, I am likely to acknowledge the constraint even if I refuse to respect it—by the excuses I offer, the urgent reasons I invent, as I pack my bags.

Merely to stay on may not be all that I am bound to do in such a case. An example from Jewish religious law is helpful here. Members of the *kahal*, the autonomous or semiautonomous community of the Middle Ages, were bound to protest against moral or religious transgressions. They were free to leave, to look for a community where they would be more comfortable with the local practices, but not until they had protested in public and tried to change the practices at home.[12] The case is the same, I think, for those of us who are the citizens of a modern democratic state. If the republic is under external attack, we may well be bound (there are difficult arguments here) to sign up as soldiers and march off to fight its enemies. If republican values are under attack at home, we may have to join a party, movement, or campaign in defense of those values.

These would be voluntary acts, strictly speaking, so long as we were free to act differently (staying on is also a voluntary act, so long as leaving is an option). Yet when we act in these ways, we are likely to feel that we are acting under a constraint. We are doing our duty. Our actions don't fit Rousseau's famous description of being forced to be free. We are not even forced to be moral. There may be considerable social pressure to "do the right thing," but we imagine our-selves acting conscientiously, which is a mode of action simultane-ously free and unfree. How so? Because we have neither determined nor chosen the right thing that we are now bound in conscience to do. Nor were we ever informed that our tacit consent—our residence in this place, our participation in the daily round of social activities—could have this radical consequence. Living together with other people just *is* a moral engagement. It ties us up in unexpected ways.

There are times, of course, when we ought to break such ties: here, involuntary association is no different from voluntary associa-tion. Sometimes we should walk away from a group that we joined a few years ago, resign from the executive committee, disengage from our fellow members, because the group no longer serves the purposes to which we are committed or because it now serves pur-poses that we oppose. The case is much the same with groups we never joined, in which we simply found ourselves. But perhaps these two cases differ in the extent to which we are bound to hang on, to protest and resist from the inside for as long as possible. Per-haps, as I am inclined to think, there is a greater obligation in the in-voluntary case, in much the same way that we might feel obliged to argue longer with a parent, child, or sibling who is doing something terribly wrong than with a spouse. We can divorce the spouse; sep-aration from the others is harder.

Suppose that we accept this account of involuntary association as a realistic sociology: What follows for political or moral theory? Obligations follow, as I have just argued, but they are simply moral facts about the given world. And isn't it the purpose of liberal au-tonomy to challenge this givenness? Aren't we supposed to criticize the associations that we find ourselves in as a result of birth and so-cialization by asking whether we would have chosen them had we been able to choose freely? Don't we have to ask ourselves what rational and autonomous agents would have done? That's a hard question, since it seems clear that rational and autonomous agents would not have done most of the things that actual human beings have done since the dawn of history. Where should the critique begin? Most human beings, given their cultural and political education, will "choose" what they have been given. Even the rebels and revolutionaries among them are likely to oppose only some parts of the given world. To exercise true liberal autonomy, must they oppose all those parts that an imaginary set of rational agents would never have chosen?

The given world, after all, is always oppressive for at least some of its members. And how will they, how will the rest of us, recognize oppression without reference to some standard of ideal freedom, perfect autonomy? The old argument about false consciousness is really an argument about the moral epistemology of involuntary association. The claim is that the four ways of finding oneself that I have listed—in a family or a culture or a state or a moral relationship—all make for intellectual servitude. We break out of this servitude only by breaking loose from these associations and making our own way. Or we imagine ourselves breaking away and so are enabled to adopt a critical attitude toward what we are actually doing.

I don't want to deny the value of such imaginings, only to insist on other values as well. The world of involuntary association always offers some space for opposition and resistance, and it also, most of the time, gives us reasons for operating within that space rather than moving wholly outside it. These reasons include loyalty to particular people, the sense of being at home with those people, the richness of a received tradition, and the longing for generational continuity. Men and women who choose to operate within a given association are not necessarily victims of false consciousness—and critics from the outside must make sure that they themselves understand the reasons for the others' choice. An informed and realistic moral sociology is the necessary precondition for a decent social criticism.

There aren't many examples of outside criticism by critics committed to this kind of sociological understanding. I will cite only one, provided by the American feminist political theorist Nancy Hirschmann, who has written a finely nuanced analysis of the practice of veiling in Muslim culture, based on accounts by Muslim women, some of them living "inside," some "outside."[13] Hirschmann describes how the veil can be an assertion of independence and a symbol of resistance—even though it originally signified, *and still does signify*, the subordination of the women who wear it. Veiling, much like the historical forms of marriage, is an inherited practice that would probably not be chosen by free women choosing from scratch. But there is no such thing as choosing from scratch; there are no absolute beginnings. The most important alternative choice for Muslim women in the modern world is, I suppose, Western liberalism (which I would certainly defend if I were speaking to them). But they may not recognize themselves as Western liberals, and there are probably customary or conventional liberal practices that they wouldn't choose if they were choosing from scratch. And so they often struggle with the practice of veiling and the subordination it represents, on the one hand, and with the "cultural imperialism" of the West, on the other. Wearing the veil, or modifying it, or wearing it sometimes, may all be meaningful choices in those struggles, which take place, inevitably, in a world of meanings that the women haven't chosen.

In this case, as in many others, the struggle against inequality and subordination within involuntary associations cannot be won by individual escape (although escape should always be available to individuals who seek it). Similarly, the struggle against economic, religious, or racial inequality in the larger society can't be won by abolishing classes, faith communities, or races. The Marxist vision of a classless society has often been generalized to religion and race. In fact, it probably isn't the right vision even for the economy. The collective improvement of the wages, working conditions, political effectiveness, and social standing of the working class is more helpful to ordinary workers than the ideological commitment to class-lessness is likely to be. That's why union activists commonly argue that the solidarity obligations of class members are more important than their mobility rights. Mobility tends to undercut solidarity and to make political organization harder; still, its appeal is strong. It may not have the same appeal, however, in other given groups, racial and religious in character, whose members seem more strongly committed to fight for collective recognition and empowerment than class members are.

Most members of racial and religious associations don't think themselves free to leave; they don't want to see their group dissolved, themselves assimilated, into the larger society. They hope to sustain the traditions they value, but in better circumstances, within a more egalitarian setting, not to abandon the traditions for the sake of equality. Nor do they want their children set loose from the traditions, required to form their own identities freely—as if children started from some mythical point zero, without a family, a culture, a country, of their own. The parents aim at a version of freedom and equality that is compatible with collective as well as individual difference. This is one of the legitimate aims—there are also illegitimate ones—of what is today called "identity politics." It follows from what the German philosopher Iring Fetscher has called "*das recht man selbst zu bleiben*"—a right to be true to oneself that holds even against, or precisely against, assimilationist campaigns waged in the name of political universalism (like state-supported efforts in the early twentieth century to "Americanize" immigrants to the United States).[14] The defense of this right plays an important part in contemporary social conflicts, which are often focused on demands for recognition and empowerment from members of involuntary associations.

Can we really imagine individuals without any involuntary ties at all, unbound by class, ethnicity, religion, race, or gender, unidentified, utterly free? The thought experiment is especially useful right now, since postmodern (late-twentieth-century) theorists have written so excitedly about "self-fashioning," an enterprise undertaken not exactly from an absolute beginning or in a social vacuum but rather—so we are told—amid the ruins of conventional social forms. I suspect that the effort to describe a *society* of self-fashioning individuals is necessarily self-defeating. But it will be interesting to see exactly where the defeats come and how definitive they are. So let's try to picture men and women like those described by the French psychoanalyst Julia Kristeva, who determine their identities and memberships "through lucidity rather than fate."[15] They decide for themselves on their life plans, choose not only their associates but the very form of their association, question every standard social pattern, recognize no bonds that they have not themselves forged. They make their lives into purely personal projects; they are entrepreneurs of the self.

This self-creation is, no doubt, "uncertain, risky, and arduous," as George Kateb, one of its advocates among American political theorists, admits.[16] But the people whose project it is would begin it as children; they would have time to grow accustomed to its difficulties. Presumably their parents—self-created men and women do have parents—would help prepare them for the choices they would have to make. Remember, we are imagining a society of such people, not simply a random set. How would the young be educated in a society like that? What exactly is involved in turning vulnerable and dependent children into free, self-making individuals?

I imagine the children being taught the values of individuality: the meaning of autonomy and integrity, the joys of free choice, the excitement of risk-taking in personal relationships and political engagements. But lessons of this sort cannot be delivered only as commands: Choose freely! Do your own thing! They are probably best conveyed in narrative form, so the children would also be told stirring stories about how a society of free individuals was created against fierce communitarian or religious opposition and how earlier, more primitive, organic or tyrannical social arrangements were escaped or overthrown. We must also assume that celebratory occasions would be lifted from these narratives and marked annually with ritual enactments of the struggle against involuntary association. This is a training for the emotions, but since the mind, too, must be readied for freedom, students would probably also be assigned required reading: the basic texts that explain and defend free individuality and the classic novels and poems written by free individuals.

All this seems to me necessary. One doesn't prepare children for any sort of human social life, let alone a life that is uncertain, risky, and arduous, by letting them run free, like wild horses on the range. On the other hand, the image of corralled horses suggests nothing so much as involuntary association, which is exactly what a school is, even a school devoted to freedom. But if schooling is necessary (and necessarily coercive), it is by no means sure to succeed. For most of these children, finding a way to express their unique individuality would likely be a strain; they would long for a conventional pattern into which they could fit themselves. In principle, however, they could be given nothing more than a general account of what an individual life plan should look like; they couldn't be told what their own plans should be. How, then, could they choose their own way? I imagine the cohort of adolescent individuals-in-the-making swept by waves of fashionable and earnest eccentricity. I imagine them rushing in and out of a great variety of associations. But would they in the end, for all the efforts of their parents and teachers, be any more differentiated, any more individualized, than the children of committed Jews or Catholics, say, or strongly identified Bulgarians or Koreans? Would they be any more tolerant of someone in their peer group who chose not to do the done thing, not to create himself by himself, herself by herself, and who announced to scandalized friends, "I am just going to copy the life plan of my parents"?

The greater number of children would not rebel in this way and

hence would constitute in time something like a "herd of independent minds" (which is how the American social critic Harold
Rosenberg described the Western intelligentsia of the 1940s and
1950s).[17] They would be proud of whatever differences they managed to cultivate and comfortable in the society of others like themselves. They would join voluntarily in the politics of that society—
although exactly how politics would work if everyone was trying to
be, or trying to appear to be, a dissident and an outsider, I am not
sure. In any case, they would surely feel bound to defend the regime
that defended their dissidence—especially against threats that
came from people proclaiming a collective commitment and common identity. Individuals would be free to leave, but not when individuality itself was under attack.

What this fictional account suggests, I think, is that there
couldn't be a society of free individuals without a socialization process, a culture of individuality, and a supportive political regime
whose citizens were prepared to be supportive in their turn. In
other words, the society of free individuals would be, for most of its
members, an involuntary association. All the social, cultural, political, and moral ties that exist in other societies would exist in this
one, too, and would have the same mixed effects, producing con-
formity and occasional rebellion.

Both the existence and legitimacy of these ties are more likely to
be denied by people who think that they are living in a radically free
society, especially by the conformists among them. And denial is
dangerous; it makes the moral and sociological analysis of involuntary association harder than it would otherwise be. We won't be able
to argue about whether the ties are too tight or too loose, whether
they require official sponsorship, or legal regulation, or private support, or active opposition, or benign neglect. We won't be able to
understand the forms of inequality produced by involuntary association or to judge (or usefully join) the struggles that go on within associations. We won't be able to acknowledge the strains of identity

politics or to distinguish reasonable from unreasonable demands for recognition and empowerment. All these things are important. Because the character of involuntary association is by no means wholly determined, it is subject to political modification. We can't modify it, however, until we recognize it. If no one is out there but fully autonomous individuals, political decisions about constraint and freedom, subordination and equality, would have no plausible object.

Critical decisions do, in fact, have to be made about all the unchosen structures, patterns, institutions, and groupings. The character and quality of involuntary associations shape the character and quality of voluntary associations in significant ways. What is involuntary is historically and biographically prior; it is the inevitable background of any social life, free or unfree, equal or unequal. We move toward freedom when we make opposition and escape possible, when we allow internal dissent and resistance, divorce, conversion, withdrawal, and resignation. We move toward equality when we open paths for social change within involuntary associations, for status realignments among them, and for redistribution across them. But mass escape is never possible; nor will realignment and redistribution ever lead to abolition. We can't bring the unchosen background wholly into the foreground, make it a matter of individual self-determination. The point is obvious, I think, but still worth stating: free choice depends on the experience of involuntary association and on the understanding of that experience, and so does egalitarian politics. Without that experience and understanding, no individuals would be strong enough to face the uncertainties of freedom, nor would there be clear and coherent alternatives among which to choose or political protection against the enemies of free choice. Even the minimal trust that makes voluntary association possible would never develop. So there wouldn't be a struggle for equality that encompassed men and women with identities and loyalties, comrades and commitments—there wouldn't be a realistic or sustainable egalitarianism.

We can work on the social background, arguing about what is necessary in different times and places, to encourage a lively engagement in associational activity and to equalize its conditions. We can, for example, improve public schools in this way or that, alter the curriculum, impose national standards or establish local control, raise the pay and prestige of teachers. We can require all children to attend these schools, or we can allow but regulate private and parochial schooling. Socialization is always coercive, but its character and conditions are open to democratic debate and reform. Similarly, we can redistribute income and opportunities for the sake of greater equality, not only among individuals but also among racial and religious groups. We can change the marriage laws, make divorce easier or more difficult, provide family allowances, interfere on behalf of battered wives and neglected children, revise our conceptions of gender roles inside and outside the family. We can alter the legal frame within which corporate or union bylaws are written, subsidize some, but not other, associations. We can ban associational rituals and practices, such as polygamy or female circumcision. We can rethink the rights and responsibilities of resident aliens. We can make military service voluntary or compulsory, exempt this or that category of men or women, and so on. Dealing with the constraints of family, ethnicity, class, race, and gender is, in large measure, what democratic politics is about. It isn't possible to abolish involuntary association; indeed, we will at times want to strengthen it, for democratic citizenship is one of the identities it can foster. Nor is there any one correct balance of the voluntary and the involuntary; we have to negotiate the proportions to meet the needs of the hour.

In practice, the results of this negotiation are less like a simple balance than a doubled mix of the two elements. The necessary background is only partly involuntary, since exit from various memberships is possible (though sometimes difficult). And the foregrounded associations—all our parties, movements, and unions—are voluntary only in a qualified sense: they represent the free choices of men and women who have been taught to make, and enabled to make, choices of just this kind . . . freely. Indeed, some of them prove the freedom by refusing to make the conventional choices. The teaching and the enabling represent the ongoing construction of this freedom: sometimes they improve upon it, sometimes they distribute its benefits more fairly, but they never produce a perfect autonomy. This limited voluntarism is immensely valuable in any case. We ought to call it freedom simply, without qualification: it is the only freedom that men and women like you and me can ever know.

In this first chapter, I have described the ways individual freedom is constrained by the realities of communal life—and it has been my intention to justify some of the constraints, to argue against an exaggerated and asocial account of what freedom is and how it works, and to begin to defend a version of equality that pays attention to men and women in groups. In the next chapter, I want to pay closer attention to the role that groups of different kinds play in the distribution of political power. When we stand alone in the voting booth, democratic citizens are exercising power in the radically individualist way that liberal theory is most comfortable with (even if we are probably voting for the party of our parents). But there are many other moments in the political process when we are only able to exercise power along with other people and when the extent of the power we exercise depends on those others. Some of us are powerful and some of us are powerless because of the groups to which we belong.

TWO

The Collectivism of Powerlessness

P OWER IS THE CURRENCY OF POLITICS, THE UNI-
versal medium that makes all things possible. It necessarily figures even in liberal political science, which
might more comfortably occupy itself with argument,
deliberation, and consent. From the outset, liberal
writers and activists aimed at limiting power. They
began by challenging kings but aimed to set limits everywhere, even
(sometimes especially) on the collective decisions of the "people."
They agreed early on that the best way to set limits was to divide
and disperse the capacity to exercise power. The famous separation of the three branches of government, described in *The Federalist,* required the existence of distinct institutional locations from
which decisions could be made, challenged, or constitutionally
overruled.[1]

Getting the separation of powers right was commonly taken by
liberals to be a matter of constitutional design: the best design made

the best regime. In classical Greece, by contrast, arguments about the best regime focused on the social order as a whole. The best regime was the political realization of the best society. The critical question about the location of power had what we might think of as a socio-logical form: Should power in the best regime/society lie with the one, the few, or the many—or with some mix of the three? Modern liberals, by contrast, aimed at a politics largely independent of soci-ety, a constitutional arrangement that would fit, and if necessary provide remedies for, a variety of social orders. For them the rele-vant questions had to do with political engineering. How should power be divided among the branches and levels of government? What range of social and economic issues fall within the jurisdiction of each, and how should disputes among them be resolved? When exactly should each of them act in the overall sequence of legislative proposal, enactment, enforcement, and review? How are their offi-cials chosen and for what term of office? Whose advice and consent is required before something can be done? Who has powers of in-vestigation and judgment after the fact?

The answers to these questions yield a constitutional system (whether or not there is a written constitution). And then the system has to be critically appraised. Do its arrangements work? Are they effective in preventing the arbitrary exercise of power? Is decision-making really divided among the three branches? These are good liberal questions; it will always be necessary to ask them. But the triumph of democracy invites more radical questions, which look back to the Greek argument about the one, the few, and the many.

Democracy is, at least in principle, the ultimate dispersal of po-litical power: each citizen, as Rousseau argued, has a $1/n$ share of "sovereign authority," where n is the total number of citizens.[2] Rousseau's fraction is both a mathematical symbol, suggesting a de-terminate part of an imagined quantity of power, and a political symbol, suggesting the equality of citizens; I shall play with both its senses. In principle, no democratic citizen has more than $1/n$ power, except with the agreement of a majority of his or her fellows, each of whom is counted equally. This is the rule of the many, even if there are constitutional limits on what the many can do; and it depends on the existence of a society in which the many are prepared to rule, endowed, that is, with the necessary education and resources. In fact, this ultimate dispersal of power has never been realized. Social and economic inequality confounds democratic principle. It is the few who really rule behind a facade of democracy—as it is commonly and most often rightly said. Hence a new set of questions arises, designed to penetrate the facade: Who makes the decisions that are ostensibly made by the people? How and where are those decisions made? Under what sorts of pressure, subject to whose influence?[3]

Liberal political scientists generally respond by arguing that although power is dispersed unequally, it is nonetheless widely dispersed. Despite the existing social and economic hierarchies, liberal democracies are mixed regimes. Some decisions are made by the one, some by the few, but many by the many—or at least in ways that take the views of the many into account. The combined effects of constitutional design and democratic politics preclude the entrenchment of particular groups or interests in power positions. Intragovernmental rivalry (between legislators and judges, for example, or between federal and local officials), periodic elections, party competition, free speech—all these combine to make decisions uncertain. Power and influence fluctuate. The political pendulum swings back and forth. The level of interest and activity among the many rises, falls, and rises again. The victories of the few are always insecure.

Even if liberals believe that all this is more or less true, the enthusiastic democrats among them, arguing that more is better, regularly come forward with suggestions for constitutional improvement and political reform: referendum and recall, proportional representation, limits on executive patronage, federal funding of political campaigns, and so on. Such measures, their proponents claim, would make for greater equality in decisionmaking, greater uncertainty about what decisions will be made, wider swings of the political pendulum, higher and more sustained levels of popular participation.

These liberal arguments and proposals have provoked a radical response (my history is schematic and only roughly chronological). Writers on the farther left of American politics claim that both the existing dispersal of power as liberals describe it and the hope for greater equality are illusory. Either the ruling class really rules, or a power elite, drawn from different classes but committed to the social and economic status quo, makes all the key decisions. Government is in principle democratic, in (liberal) theory mixed, and in practice oligarchic. Elections are a sideshow, not a dispersal of power but a diversion from and a mystification of its actual coherence. Ordinary citizens passively accept their subordination, or they resist only at the margins, or they join mass movements that somehow always fail. The victories that liberal or left parties celebrate are always minor, allowed or even designed by the elite to accommodate discontented groups and co-opt their leaders. Immense effort produces marginal reform.

Some radical critics have argued further that the liberal focus on constitutionalism and decisionmaking (and therefore on programs enacted or defeated, reforms won or lost) is a mistake. What is crucial is the decision that isn't made, the proposal that is never considered, the innovative idea that is somehow always out of the question. Ruling a country means controlling the political agenda, defining what is thinkable and unthinkable, and this work is always done behind the facade of democratic politics.[4] We the people debate the range of thinkable policies with great freedom, believing that our options are open. But the critical alternatives never come up; they lie somewhere beyond the democratic horizon.

More severely structuralist critiques of liberalism arguably provide the best version of this radical position. These focus not so much on the exercise of power, on whether to make decisions or rule them out of consideration, but on its possession. (I will talk more about possession than exercise in the rest of this chapter, but I don't mean to enter into these theoretical debates.) Where is power located within the social system? Who has the potential, the power, to act? Because this version of the radical critique has been heavily influenced by Marxist theory, it focuses above all on the power of capital, on the way that wealth is converted into political influence and, ultimately, domination, without the members of the dominant class necessarily undertaking anything that we would recognize as political decisionmaking. Now the existing regime, the object of radical opposition, is not simply an oligarchy; it is a plutocracy—an impersonal plutocracy, however, in which capital itself rules and all the rest of us play our assigned parts.

Liberal reformers have also addressed the question of money in politics. Even if they don't acknowledge its invisible, structural, regime-determining effects, they are keenly aware of its everyday effectiveness. They see its visible power in the bribery of public officials, the virtual purchase of electoral office through campaign contributions, the ownership of the communications media, and so on. And they aren't unaware—most of them, anyway—of its more indirect uses: to bring the police into labor disputes, to shape governmental trade and financial policies, to shift tax burdens and minimize or reverse legislative efforts at redistribution. The direct uses of money require a direct political response: a ban on bribery, the establishment of civil service exams, the reform of campaign finances. The indirect uses require something else, which can be achieved only in part through constitutional design or legislative reform: the establishment of "countervailing" powers in society to match and offset the power of wealth.[5] Countervalence is, in a way, a response to the structuralist critique of liberalism. It makes for an informal constitutionalization of social life; as the state is divided and balanced, so is civil society. Groups opposed to the plutocrats seek and sometimes achieve the power to challenge their decisions.

Countervailing power can take many forms, but if it is to serve the purposes of democratic politics, it has to engage the many against the few. In the modern world, this has most often meant to organize labor against capital. The conflict of unions and corporations, where the state is commonly enlisted on the corporate side, requires instead a tilt in favor of labor. Here is the prime example of countervalence; and the redistributive effects of collective bargaining, particularly in the late 1940s and 1950s, provide the best evidence of its success. But other forms of powerlessness can also be accommodated by this model—at least this is the claim of liberal political theorists. Marginalized and pariah groups, even if they are racially or religiously rather than economically marked, can also be organized to defend themselves and advance their common interests. They can become part of the overall system of countervalence and social constitutionalism, which consists of many different groups working sometimes alone, sometimes in coalition, to balance and constrain the most powerful among them.

The aim of liberal countervalence is still the democratic dispersal of power to individual men and women, the delivery to each of his or her $1/n$ power. Interest groups are simply the instruments of this delivery. And, in truth, radical critics of liberalism do not have a different end in view, for a society in which the full democratic dispersal of power was realized would also be the classless society of the Marxist vision. Both the liberal and the radical visions involve the dissolution of the categories of difference for the sake of an equality that is measured one individual at a time—each one compared with each other one to ensure $1/n$ for all. One person, one vote, one quantum of influence and power. The key disagreement between liberals and radicals is not over the importance of all these "ones" but over the difficulty of achieving their equality. Against the persistent optimism of liberal reformers, radicals insist that their structural analysis of capitalist societies demonstrates that equality cannot be served by countervailing interest groups but only by a movement for social transformation. Interest groups can be bought off or, if necessary, constrained and repressed. Only a revolutionary movement can challenge the rule of the ruling class.

I don't want to underestimate the force of this radical critique, even if, after 1989, no one is defending its strongest version. Inequality in capitalist societies is systemic, and the system is very strongly established. Liberal reforms have produced only limited victories; like the unionization campaigns of the 1930s, they are often themselves dependent on radical energies and ambitions. Nonetheless, there have been real victories; real defeats, too. The pendulum swings that liberal constitutionalism predicts have actually occurred. For extended periods of time, participation in democratic politics has dramatically increased, and income and power gaps have narrowed, sometimes significantly. Radical structural analysis does not fare well in explaining these victories; its advocates tend instead, as I have already suggested, to deny or minimize the value of whatever gains have been made. It represents a refusal to come to grips with the experience of subjection and (partial) liberation. Many radical critics have been unwilling to acknowledge, for example, the changes in life on the factory floor that unionization brought: not equality, to be sure, but the end of the arbitrary power of foremen and managers, which was also the end of humiliation and oppression as ordinary workday realities (they return, of course, when union power declines).[6]

Victories of this sort are enormously important, and not only because they enhance the quality of life for millions of people. Egalitarianism, even when it stops short of $1/n$ for everyone, limits the power of the most powerful groups. Rousseau's fraction suggests a universal sharing of political power, which is a regulative ideal not likely to be realized anytime soon. But every move in the direction of equality has the immediate effect of setting limits on what can be done by those who have more than $1/n$. Countervalence is a general idea that covers a range of necessary democratic activities: opposition, resistance, protest, and collective bargaining.

So we have to attend carefully to the liberal model, which at least explains important accomplishments like those of the labor movement. I suggest that we call it the "emancipation" model. Here is how it works, given a more or less democratic political order. Members of oppressed groups are first granted citizenship, which turns out to be a formal, not yet fully effective allocation of political power. Then, slowly, they organize themselves into a movement or interest group, pooling their power and learning to exercise it in a disciplined way. They aim in the long run at equal power, $1/n$, in the larger society, but they achieve an immediate enhancement of their power position because the first relevant n is—to stick with our example—the number of unionized workers, and, as the old song goes, "The union makes us strong." They get stronger by forming coalitions with other groups or by attracting the support of existing political parties. They challenge their oppressors at the point of oppression—the factory floor, the segregated lunch counter, the residential neighborhood "protected" by restrictive covenants—and then at the ballot box. They exploit the checks and balances of the liberal constitutional system, working sometimes at the state level, sometimes at the federal level, finding support in Congress, in the courts, or among civil servants.

Gradually but steadily, their members acquire the competence and accumulate the resources necessary for democratic success, and they gain the self-confidence that comes from succeeding. Finally, they complete their emancipation by escaping not only from oppression but also from the oppressed group. Now they are individual men and women, no longer subject to the discipline of a movement. They don't have anything quite like $1/n$ power—that equality still lies in the distant future—but they have more power than they started with, and they deploy it as they please. They, or their children, are agents of social, geographic, and political mobility. They climb up the income and status hierarchy, they move out of the old neighborhood, they join and leave political parties—always carrying their power with them. They participate in the system of countervalence, but not necessarily with their original group. They are freely mobile in civil society.

This liberal model accounts for a lot of what has happened in the United States over the past century. Many Americans will recognize in it their own family history, or an idealized version of it. But many others will not. If radical analysis doesn't explain the successes of emancipation, the liberal model doesn't explain the failures; it doesn't help us understand what Charles Tilly calls "durable inequality."[7] Why have some people or, more accurately, some groups been left so far behind?

The deepest and most enduring inequalities are not primarily economic in their origins. They have their roots in cultural and racial/ethnic differences and in the political exploitation of these differences. Nor are they amenable to liberal emancipation in its standard version, because overcoming them requires something very different from the temporary pooling and then the wide dispersal of political power. The objects of durable inequality are a special subclass of the involuntary associations that I described in the first chapter of this book; they are "categorical" and stigmatized groups. In the United States today these are, most importantly, racial groups, blacks and Native Americans; in other times and places ethnicity and religion have made for similar inequalities. Neither classlessness nor individual autonomy, admirable as these ideals are, suggests an effective remedy for stigmatization and the oppression it commonly entails.

Liberal and radical theories are equally inadequate in dealing with this kind of oppression. The oppressed group is not like the Marxist working class, nor is it like any of the liberal interest groups:

it is not a collection of individuals who have made their way into the class or the group by their own paths, one person or family at a time. The members of stigmatized groups are not individuals held together only by the disadvantages they share, who become a coherent collective with a common consciousness only through political action and who have no reason to remain together once their politics is successful. In the real world of durable inequality, individuals do not become members of these groups because they are disadvantaged; they are disadvantaged because they are members.[8] Membership *is* the disadvantage. The members are categorized and stigmatized collectively, not individually, and then they are systematically discriminated against socially and economically. According to the classic liberal understanding of the market, people rise and fall, succeed or fail, one by one; stigma, by contrast, is a common fate.

Why won't the emancipation model work for stigmatized groups? We can get some sense of the reasons if we look at the history of empire and the experience of national liberation. Consider the Algerian Arabs at the moment when, belatedly, they were offered equal rights with French citizens and the prospect of full-scale inclusion in the republic. In Algeria before that, the European colonists had dominated both society and economy (although there were plenty of poor *pied noirs*); the Arabs were the "natives," regarded as backward, uneducated, superstitious, lazy, and so on—these stereotypes are not highly differentiated across colonial settings. There were exceptions, of course; some European leftists tried to organize political movements that could draw people from both sides of the existing ethnic/national line. But basically the Arabs were a subordinate and stigmatized group, despised by the colonizers.[9]

Citizenship would have set them on the road to emancipation— a long road, no doubt, but one that led, according to all the signposts, to an assured destination: equal standing with the Europeans in Algeria and with ordinary French men and women in all the other provinces of the republic. The vast majority of Algerian Arabs, however, chose another road. They didn't want to be individually French; they wanted to be collectively Arab and perhaps also collectively Muslim. The stigmatized identity was also a valued identity, and few people were ready to abandon it. This reluctance is common among members of involuntary associations, for reasons I have already discussed, but it takes on a passionate intensity among pariah, colonized, and stigmatized groups (even if there are also individuals trying to break away and shed the stigma). Nor did the Algerians believe—nor were they encouraged to believe by the signposts on the road to citizenship, which were all in French—that they could retain their identity and still become equal citizens of the republic. In *that* republic, they believed, they would be unequal for the duration. And so they chose national liberation over liberal emancipation. Most of the world readily accepted their choice, in part because they were a conquered people, anciently established on territory that was distinct and conveniently separated from the territory of the French. The precondition of citizenship was assimilation, and almost no one expected Arabs in Algeria to assimilate into the French people. (I will come in a moment to the different, but not entirely different, question of Arabs in France.)

It turns out, then, that when we think about $1/n$ power, we have to think of n not only as a number but also as a group: n isn't 100,000 simply, but 100,000 somebodies—Arabs or French people or Russians or Chinese. And in cases like the Algerians', the value of the fraction depends not only on the numerical value of n but also on what n it is, and then on the character and quality, the pride, prestige, and material wealth, of the collective it represents. The liberation movement isn't merely instrumental now, a temporary pooling of resources aimed at eventual inclusion in a larger and less determinate body; it has a value in and of itself, created by the historical and contemporary investment of its members in the nation. In everyday arithmetic, the value of a fraction gets smaller as the de-

nominator gets larger; in the political arithmetic of national liberation, the two can advance together. I am a more powerful person
when I am a member, of a larger, more resourceful, more competent,
and more successful group, even though I am still only one member.
The way to make Algerians the equals of the French is to create an
attractive and prosperous Algerian state alongside the French state.
Or, better, that's the necessary first step toward equality.

So emancipation and national liberation are different in this
crucial way. In the second case, the oppressed group doesn't dis-
solve into the larger society; instead, it consolidates its own "group-
ness." But national liberation assumes a society of states, within
which consolidation takes the form of sovereignty. Within a single
state, emancipation would seem to be the preferred model. What
about Arabs in France, then, some of whom are now French citizens? They pool their resources in a variety of organizations that
work toward full equality, and they participate in labor unions and
left political parties that claim to have the same end in view. Won't
they soon be both emancipated and assimilated? Maybe, but there is
a lot of evidence suggesting that for a long time to come they will
occupy, as a group and not merely as a collection of unfortunate individuals, the lowest ranks of the social hierarchy. If we insist on
asking the radical questions How is power dispersed? How are decisions made? we will discover that individual Arabs, even if they
are citizens of the French republic, don't possess as much power as
ethnically French citizens. Again, this is the result of their collective identity; it can't be understood as individual failure or misfor-
tune serially reiterated.[10] Arabs in France would certainly be helped
by left-wing political success—but not enough, probably, to bring
them to full equality.

What is necessary in cases like this is a version of collective empowerment. But this version has to be compatible with, has to sit,
even if a little uncomfortably, alongside, emancipation and citizenship. I don't want to replace the liberal model, only to supplement

it. Given the existence of racial, ethnic, and religious (in addition to class) hierarchies, given categorical inequality, the empowerment of individuals will come not simply by way of but permanently conjoined with the empowerment of groups. How to make that conjunction work, how to make it compatible with democratic politics, seems to me a central question for the contemporary left—or for anyone who continues to care about equality.

The hardest case of categorical inequality hasn't yet figured in my argument and may not fit the empowerment model that I now mean to defend. The gender hierarchy is the most ancient and enduring form of inequality—"hardest," then, because it has survived so many social transformations. Certainly women have been, in all the civilizations that I know about, a stigmatized group (even when an ideal image of womankind is made the object of poetic adoration). I am sure that the stigmas show some cultural variation, but what is most interesting, indeed, amazing, is how standard they are across many cultures. Women are conventionally described—by men—as emotional, irrational, mentally and morally weak, sexually driven, readily distracted from any serious activity.[11] On the basis of these descriptions, they are or until very recently have been excluded from positions of power; except for a few aristocratic women, a few queens and empresses, they have played hardly any role in public decisionmaking.

But if, when the phrase *stigmatized group* is applied to women, the adjective is easy to explain, the noun raises many difficulties. In contrast to all the other groups that I have been considering, women do not share a cultural or religious life separate from that of men; they don't inhabit a distinct territory or district or neighborhood; they don't have a history that can be disentangled from the history of men or, better, from history generally. They live mostly in families, and their culture and religion (like their social class) are usually no different from those of their fathers, brothers, husbands, and sons. I don't mean that there wasn't a culture of women in medieval Christendom or ancient China, or that there isn't one in contemporary Islam or America today. But there isn't a culture of women that transcends these different worlds and exists coherently outside them. Instead, women are integrated into the surrounding culture, which is also their own. More than this, they are the primary agents of cultural reproduction. But the culture that they reproduce is not peculiarly their own; they socialize their sons and daughters into the common culture, Arab, Muslim, French, Christian, whatever.

That women are radically dispersed in homes and families is the special feature of their historical powerlessness. Dispersal is the ideal end of the emancipation process, when we imagine many individuals, male and female, moving freely about in political and civil society, each with his or her own $1/n$ power share. But dispersal is dangerously incapacitating at the beginning of emancipation, as Marx understood when he wrote his famous argument about how the concentration of workers in cities and factories would make revolutionary politics possible. Women are never concentrated in that way; they live among men, most of them with men. For this reason, mass organization and revolutionary politics have been difficult, if not impossible, for them. The women's movement has made significant gains in recent years, but these gains have been won along lines suggested by the liberal emancipation model. The success of the fight for full citizenship and suffrage set the stage for the formation of interest groups that address particular grievances, chiefly legal and economic, and for a political mobilization aimed above all at increasing the number of women in public office. Both of these fights have been partially successful, and the result has been the entrance of more and more women into leadership positions in both the corporate and political worlds.[12] These entrances are achieved one by one, but in their wake the general position of women has also improved; now they possess something closer to their democratic entitlement of $1/n$ power than they have ever possessed before. But what this n designates is so many millions of adult American citizens. Emancipated women don't become, and don't seek to become, the agents of a more narrow self-determination, not even within the larger setting of American democracy. Insofar as the ancient stigmas are erased, they live as ordinary citizens; if they participate in cultures of difference, they do so as blacks, or Jews, or Latinas far more often than as women.

At least, this is what appears to be happening. The test will be whether emancipated women feel any need for a permanent and separate institutional life. Will the "civil service" of the contemporary women's movement survive the success of that movement? Would a career in women's institutions have any appeal if the common institutions of American life were equally open, at the top as well as in the lower ranks, to competent and ambitious women? I am unsure how to answer these questions, but comparable questions about other categorical and stigmatized groups seem to me easy to answer. When blacks have finally achieved equal standing in the American economy and in society generally, there will still be black churches, black neighborhoods, black organizations for mutual aid, black magazines, cultural societies, and educational institutions. The case of the Jews, I believe, will prove typical for other pariah groups: there are now Jewish senators, governors, and mayors; there are Jewish CEOs of major corporations; still, a career in the Jewish civil service, in the synagogues, federations, congresses, and committees that make up the separate organizational life of American Jewry and provide life-cycle services to American Jews, seems attractive and rewarding to many people. We need to understand why this is so, for it points the way to an egalitarian politics that might be helpful in meeting the challenge of durable inequality.

Class and culture are not entirely distinct categories, but we can learn a lot from their differences. By and large, in the United States today, class organizations do not seek to provide life-cycle services to their members, so they do not develop anywhere near as rich an institutional life as cultural (most importantly, religious) groups do. Nor is their civil service committed to its own permanence. Interest groups often outlast the interests they represent, but in principle they are not supposed to. The organizations of the Marxist working class provide the classic example. Since their activists look forward, in theory at least, to the creation of a classless society, they also look forward to the dissolution of their own movements, parties, newspapers, and youth groups. European social democracy was, for a time, an exception to this theoretical rule: its leaders did not really believe in classlessness (or in revolution), so they set about consolidating working-class culture; they tried to provide the full gamut of life-cycle services, from nursery schools to burial societies. But social mobility and cultural democratization have had effects like those that revolution was supposed to have, making it impossible to reproduce the collective life of the working class. The success of social democracy undercuts its own culture.

By contrast, religious groups generally, and some racial and ethnic groups, have managed to control their means of cultural reproduction and to provide extensive life-cycle services. But they have not managed equally well. Inequalities that endure from generation to generation are the consequence of the radically uneven success of majority and minority, central and peripheral, dominant and subordinate cultures. There is probably further unevenness within the set of minority, peripheral, and subordinate groups, but I am going to ignore that for now in order to make a crucial point about all of them together. These groups are marked not only by the poverty of their individual members but also by their collective incapacity to accumulate resources and provide crucial services: schooling, welfare, loans, mutual defense. Stigmatized and pariah groups do reproduce themselves, socializing their children and celebrating the key moments of birth, adulthood, marriage, childbearing, and death. They sustain their common life—but they cannot improve or advance it.

They suffer from a double deficit: it isn't just that the poverty of individuals adds up to the poverty of the group; group poverty confirms and intensifies the effects of individual poverty. The problem of durable inequality needs to be addressed at both levels.

In the literature of community and multiculturalism, it is commonly said that what stigmatized groups need is "recognition," which is either the public erasure of the stigma or the redescription of the stigma as an honor: "Black is beautiful." Recognition is no doubt a good thing, and in the context of a long history of denigration and rejection, it may well be necessary. But its value has sometimes been exaggerated in the debates about identity politics. The members of oppressed groups have been encouraged—mistakenly, I think—to believe themselves injured above all by the disrespect of the dominant others and to seek the signs of proper regard. But a permanent state of suspicion about the demeaning or malicious things that are about to be said or done is self-defeating. It leads too often to a dead-end politics of anger and resentment.

It is probably also self-defeating to imagine that the long-term goal of recognition and respect is best achieved directly, by insisting on respect itself. (Indeed, the insistence is funny; the American comedian Rodney Dangerfield has made a career out of it.) Consider the analogy of happiness, which we don't achieve, despite the American Declaration of Independence, by pursuing it. We aim at goals like satisfying work and good relationships and particular pleasurable experiences, and if we find these, we are happy. Happiness is a by-product. Jon Elster has written extensively about ends of this sort, which must be achieved indirectly and for which focused effort may well be counterproductive, like trying to fall asleep.[13] People do not win respect by insisting that they are not respected enough.

What do groups need to do to escape stigmatization, to be recognized and respected? What goals should they pursue directly? They need a secure place in the world, an institutional presence, and, above all, political and economic resources. And then they need to coexist with other groups similarly placed, roughly equal to themselves. The other groups are necessary to do the recognizing and respecting, and they will want to be recognized and respected in turn. In international society, this reciprocity is supposed to be normal among states; in domestic society, it requires a conscious multiculturalism. But reciprocity won't work if it is nothing more than the coexistence of culturally identified men and women, each one nervously (and some of them obsessively) focused on the rhetoric and gestures of the others. We need what I will call "meat-and-potatoes multiculturalism," where the material strength of groups compels their mutual respect.

This strength won't be achieved by turning the group into a corporation, a legal person with collective rights and obligations. In a liberal society, groups cannot establish a corporate existence of that sort, because the state won't, and shouldn't, police their boundaries or provide them with a fixed membership, capable of choosing leaders and taxing itself for the sake of communal well-being. The standard shape of group life, given the freedom of civil society, is core plus periphery: a core of believers or activists and a larger group of members and not-quite-members, differently connected to the core, spreading into the distance, overlapping with peripheries of other cores. The test of the core is its ability to recruit time, energy, and money from some substantial part of its periphery and to fund and staff its own institutions, bureaucracies, and welfare services. When a large number of core groups can meet this test, we have meat-and-potatoes multiculturalism.[14]

The best way, perhaps the only way, to overcome durable inequality is to enable the believers or activists of stigmatized groups—like American blacks or, given the significance of religion in American life, black Baptists—to connect with their peripheries, to accumulate resources, and to provide life-cycle services similar to those provided by more advantaged groups. This is the empowerment model: It begins with individuals associated with a group and diminished by the association; it empowers them by strengthening the group. Now their power amounts to $1/n$, where n is, say, 30 million organized and newly resourceful black Americans; subsequently but also simultaneously, their power is $1/n$ over n', where n' is the total number of Americans (I make the same assumption that I made before: this isn't yet actual equality). Empowerment is still an individualist model, but it recognizes that individuals live in groups and that their place in society is determined in part by the place of their groups. Further, it seizes upon the loyalty of many individuals to a particular group, even when they are associated with more than one, to fuel an egalitarian politics. Ambition is the fuel of the emancipation model (so are the hope that ambitions can be fulfilled and the indignation that comes when they are thwarted). But ambition is only part of the individualist story, and it is overemphasized in many accounts. Attachment is the other part, and because of the power of attachment, no society of equals can be achieved or sustained without collective empowerment.[15]

I mean to make a simple and even crude argument: we won't erase the stigmas carried by the most seriously stigmatized groups in our society until they are provided with, and can provide their members with, the full range of material resources and services, which I sum up as meat and potatoes. It isn't enough to help individuals escape from stigmatized groups. A one-by-one emancipation won't work when group identity, however it looks from the outside, is valued on the inside—as it commonly is. Even when stigmatization produces self-hate among some members of a stigmatized group, the greater number will resist, sensing that self-hate is a pathology. Most people will aim to deal with the pathology by strengthening the group, not by abandoning it.

How to provide the meat and potatoes is not a question that I want to address at any length here; I will have a little more to say about it in my discussion of civil society in Chapter 4. Self-provision is best, not only by tapping group resources, which may be woefully inadequate, but also by organizing politically to tap the resources of the state. There are many ways to do this, and many ways to enhance the possibility that it will be done; when it comes to collecting and distributing money, both states and citizens have many options. But it is crucial to recognize a problem that isn't limited to stigmatized groups: all the cores and peripheries that exist in liberal societies suffer from free riders. They suffer willingly; the core provides services that it doesn't want to deny to peripheral members and not-quite-members; that's the way it attracts and holds them. But it can't tax any of its members to pay for the services. So the state has to step in, one way or another; we can argue about the best ways. And it does step in, though usually with programs that are most helpful to the most powerful, best organized, and politically most competent groups. A form of state provision designed to assist the weaker groups will be a *necessary—and permanent—*feature of any egalitarian multiculturalism.

Whatever the case with class and gender, we have every reason to think that some racial, religious, and ethnic groups will survive emancipation and will continue to need institutions and civil services of their own. Their members will continue to mark the life cycle together. Intermarriage will bring many families into more than one set of life-cycle celebrations, but I suspect that most people will make choices among the different sets. Perhaps they will drift toward the distant peripheries of, say, their parents' primary group, but they will still want to celebrate the key moments of their own and their children's lives, and these celebrations will mostly be collective in character. Culturally specific rites of passage and communal provision for times of joy and sorrow: these are especially important, I think, to members of pariah groups. And individuals who are confident that their community will make these provisions will be stronger overall—and more respected, too, because they will be running organizations, collecting and spending money (including tax money), and attending to the needs of their own people. These are the features of collective life that command respect, even when, especially when, no one is asking for respect. We can be sure, then, that mediated empowerment, $1/n$ over n', will be a feature of any egalitarian society.

The emancipation and empowerment models need to work simultaneously—with different groups (or the same group at different times) choosing one or the other. These two are necessary features of liberal politics and civil society. Sometimes they will make for countervalence, sometimes for a simple dispersal of power. But power won't always be dispersed directly to individuals; it will also be concentrated at different locations in social space, and individuals will be empowered by the concentrations. They won't, of course, be equally empowered. Liberal emancipation aims at a future society in which the equality of $1/n$ is fully achieved. The empowerment model is different, for it works by mediation, and mediation always produces inequalities; the mediating groups and institutions have different histories, political trajectories, resources, skills at the top, and so on. Nonetheless, empowerment will undermine the durable inequalities that have plagued liberal society. It will make for greater overall equality. Short of abolishing differences, as many liberals and radicals have dreamed of doing but won't ever be able to do, there is no better way to greater equality.

But the empowerment model, many liberals fear, will in the end divide and fragment America.[16] Emancipation produces citizens, whereas empowerment produces parochial communities of Jews, blacks, and Native Americans. It is true enough that in the struggle for empowerment, voices can be heard defending hard-line nationalist conceptions of communal life. But such conceptions are not likely to win, for two chief reasons. First, the members of these communities hold alternative or additional memberships, some of them in class movements and interest groups whose aim is emancipation. Second, the struggle for empowerment is waged within the world of democratic politics; it involves, among other things, a campaign for state support. If it produces, in contrast to emancipation, hyphenated Americans and a mediated citizenship, it is nonetheless true that the American side of the hyphen and the sense of being a citizen are strengthened by empowerment: that is one of its notable egalitarian effects. It contributes significantly to the sense of efficacy of the citizen-members, which is to say that it leads them to think, not wrongly, that they have more power than they had before, not only to shape their own lives within their groups but also to influence the life of the larger community.

Members of empowered groups participate in the (constitutional) political system both as citizens and as members. The best evidence for this is their voting behavior, which is strongly conditioned but not determined by their membership: some of them agree among themselves about their interests as members and vote together; some of them disagree and vote differently; and the same thing is true of their interests as citizens. The weakest groups come closest to straightforward bloc voting, although they also have low voting rates: only their active members are mobilized and disciplined for the power struggle. Further along in the struggle, if we ever get further along, emancipation and empowerment, the common work of citizens and the common work of members, will coexist more easily. They already coexist among the members of established groups—a tribute to the permanent complications of interest and identity.

Imagine a radical (structural) dispersal of political power, first, among the branches and levels of government, among all the civil servants in constitutional positions, and among citizens, with their democratically identical $1/n$ shares; and second, among all the activist cores, among the alternative civil services of America's movements and groups, and among the members they serve, spreading out to the multiple peripheries. This is, I think, a picture to be admired and a plan that we should try to realize. We don't have to give up the one, the few, and the many; the need to resist the power of the plutocratic few remains central to any egalitarian politics. But only a mediated redistribution of resources through the cores and peripheries of group life will begin to deal with the enduring inequalities that liberal egalitarianism has so far failed to address.

In the next chapter I want to look closely at a particular and highly problematic categorical group, the traditionalist ethnic or fundamentalist religious community, whose members are often stigmatized, beleaguered, and impoverished. I will consider the claims that such communities make on liberal democracies—above all, a claim that most liberals would deny if they could: that the community has a right to control totally the education of its children in order to guarantee the reproduction of its way of life. But what about the reproduction of democratic citizenship?

THREE

Cultural Rights

CULTURAL COMMUNITIES ARE INVOLUNTARY associations in exactly the sense that I suggested in the first chapter. Individuals are enrolled by their parents, and although there is considerable coming and going in subsequent years, most people hover around the groups in which they have been enrolled, sometimes drifting away from their practices and beliefs, sometimes drifting back. I want to consider one of the claims that some groups of this sort make on the larger society—a claim not (or not primarily) for material support but for "cultural rights." The negotiation of such claims often figures in the politics of recognition and empowerment. But the actual negotiations make everyone uneasy; long-standing fears and resentments, bred by isolation and inequality, come into play.

The groups that make the strongest claims are minorities whose members are committed to a traditionalist or fundamentalist version of religion and culture and are marginal, vulnerable, poor, and stigmatized, in part at least, because of that commitment. In the United States, these members make up a relatively small proportion of the victims of durable inequality; in other countries they figure more significantly. In any case, the groups they form pose especially difficult problems for the liberal state. And liberal theorists, who are unhappy with all forms of culturalist politics, worry particularly about these groups. As I suggested in the last chapter, they prefer to address inequalities in the language of class rather than community. But some inequalities really are rooted in culture and community. Class turns out to be a utopian concept.

So let's ask, What is the point of the cultural rights demanded by many minority religious and ethnic communities in the modern world? And how far should liberal democracies (or social democracies) go in accommodating communities of this kind? I mean these to be practical questions. I am not interested here in the philosophical debate about whether these rights exist and, if they do, whether groups or only individuals can be said to have them. The claims are important whether or not the rights are real. Rights talk, however, is our natural language; I will not be able to avoid it even when I insist that the way we respond to culturalist demands depends more on sociology than on philosophy. When arguing about multiculturalism and democratic citizenship, we have to pay attention, as I have only begun to do, to the specific features of group life and the specific demands of different groups.

Liberal democracies should have no difficulty acknowledging rights to communal self-organization, to religious worship and the celebration of the life cycle, to the free and open use of a traditional or national language within a community in ritual or domestic settings and possibly in some political settings, and to the public recognition of the community and its culture in museums and monuments and perhaps also in the state calendar.[1] These points are relatively easy to accept. Although some people might argue for the necessary neutrality of the state calendar, neutrality would seem to be consistent with a broad and equal fullness; a calendar that marked all the important ethnic and religious holidays would favor no particular ethnicity or religion.

However easy it is to acknowledge community self-organization and culture, the central meaning of the demand for cultural rights is not at all easy to accept. It has to do with social reproduction, which necessarily involves the coercion of children and thus encroaches on the power of the state. It forces us to confront in the strongest way the involuntariness of involuntary associations. The claim is that every racial, ethnic, religious (or, for that matter, political or ideological) community has a right to try to reproduce itself—which means the right to raise and educate its own children. The claim is made most passionately by members of weak, vulnerable, and stigmatized groups who believe that their very survival, their collective future, is in jeopardy.

"A right to try . . .": that sounds like a right that should be readily acknowledged and should pass uncontested. But it is contested, most importantly because in so much of the modern world people belong to more than one community, and so social reproduction requires that their children be taught more than one history and culture. The teachings may be inconsistent, even contradictory; and there are sure to be conflicts over which teaching takes precedence and over who, finally, is in control of the educational process. These conflicts are often wrenching for individuals, and when they are acted out politically, they often divide the community and the country in which it dwells. In certain sorts of communities—I will call them liberal communities—the conflicts can be, and indeed have been, successfully managed. But this experience may be misleading.

Imagine a case from our own country: a set of parents who are U.S. citizens, Catholics, and Italian-Americans. At every level of the educational system, these parents will have to make difficult or potentially difficult choices between public/secular and parochial/

religious schools. These are parental choices, but they are shaped, and their financial consequences are determined, by budgetary decisions made within the church and by the government of the state and town (schooling is the most decentralized governmental function in the United States). Whether the social reproduction of Catholic Italian-Americans should be funded with public money, wholly or partly or not at all, is an important and disputed political question. If public funding is provided, as it is in many European countries (though only for religious groups), the body of citizens will presumably want some say in how it is spent. The citizens will be concerned about their own reproduction. The standard democratic practice is to require that certain courses having to do with the state and its legitimacy be taught in the parochial schools that the state is paying for. In the United States, state governments impose such requirements even though they don't pay for but only license and certify the parochial schools: they commonly require courses on American history and literature and on democratic politics. And isn't it a justifiable practice for democratic citizens, exactly as it is for strongly identified Italian-Americans or faithful Catholics, to try to reproduce their values and commitments in the next generation?

Yes, it is justifiable, and it is also possible, most of the time, to arrange for the (more or less) simultaneous enactment of these different reproductive/educational activities, because each of the three communities I am now considering is a liberal community, which is to say, it is prepared to accept the divided loyalties of its members. The United States has long acknowledged the pluralism of American society and the resulting hyphenated identities of its citizens (it even permits dual citizenship and the twofold allegiance that entails). So *Italian-American* is fine with other Americans—as it is with Italians in America, whose community is very loosely structured, ready to accommodate the participation of its members in American politics and society and to accept, however unhappily, the consequences of this participation: namely, members who move away from Italianness and then sometimes return with non-Italian spouses in tow. In similar fashion, American Catholicism has gradually accommodated itself to the practices and even to the values of democratic debate and decision (despite its own hierarchical character)—so that faithful Catholics can also be Democrats and Republicans, liberals and conservatives, socialists and defenders of laissez-faire; they can even be members of ginger groups dedicated to reforming the church. These three communities—Americans, Italian-Americans, and Catholics—have been pluralized from within, and as a result, the claims they make to reproduce themselves are already qualified by a recognition of similar (but different) claims made on behalf of some or even all of their own members.[2]

The different claims have to be negotiated—and commonly they can be; they are mostly meat-and-potatoes claims. It isn't difficult to imagine the negotiations temporarily deadlocked or suspended in anger, as negotiations over the funding and regulation of parochial schools have frequently been in the United States, ever since Catholic immigrants began arriving in large numbers in the 1840s. But once Catholics recognize that their children are also future citizens of a democratic secular state, and once all the other Americans recognize that some of their fellow citizens are faithful Catholics, and once Italian-Americans recognize that their children may marry non-Italian-Americans, the hardest questions have been settled. The key to the settlement is that these communities have effectively given up any claim to the total loyalty of their members. No doubt, they still hope to capture a substantial part of the time, energy, and available wealth of their members, but they don't demand everything.

This is exactly the situation that the political theorist David Miller describes with a different example, arguing that there is no conflict between an Arab ethnic identity and a French national/republican identity.[3] That is true as long as the two make room for each other. Some militant Muslims and some modern-day Jacobins, however, are not willing to do that.

As long as groups don't make radical or total demands, the resulting negotiations, deadlocks and all, represent a possible liberal politics. Divided loyalties open the way for individual choice, and although liberal philosophers may worry about the extent to which these choices are determined by ethnic or religious commitments that are inherited rather than deliberated, they can make their peace with the kind of pluralism I have been describing. It also turns out to be relatively easy to move resources across the boundaries of these pluralized and divided communities. The redistributive project of contemporary liberalism is at least consistent with the ongoing collective life of Catholics and Italian-Americans.

Consider now a radically different kind of collective life, largely undreamt of in liberal philosophy. Some years ago, the sociologist Lewis Coser published a book called *Greedy Institutions,* in which he examined groups and organizations that did in fact demand everything (or almost everything—*everything* is a relative term) that their members could give.[4] Most of the groups discussed in Coser's book recruited their members as adults; the Communist Party as it once was, is an obvious example. But people are also born and bred in greedy or totalizing communities. The members of such communities or, better, their children, inherit (rather than choose) a social system that is complete in every detail and that includes, in all the important cases, a place for each of them in a fully developed hierarchy: men and women, old and young, learned and ignorant.

The key purpose of education in such a community is to teach future members the duties of their place. And it is this narrow and exclusive focus that makes the right of social reproduction so problematic—problematic, I mean, for a liberal and democratic society, but only in liberal, democratic societies are claims made in the language of rights. Here is my practical question, then: Should we (liberals and democrats) recognize the right of totalizing communities, like fundamentalist or ultraorthodox religious groups (the *haredim* in Israel; Pentecostal sects in the United States) or like traditionalist ethnic groups (the Aboriginal tribes of Canada and New Zealand), to reproduce themselves—that is, to do whatever they think necessary to pass on their way of life to their children, who are also future citizens of a democratic state? And should the state in any way support the exercise of this right?

The right is problematic for three reasons:

1. because these groups generally don't recognize the individual rights attributed equally to all their members, men and women alike, by the democratic state, so they won't be inclined to teach their members about such rights. Above all, they won't want their children to understand the full extent of their liberal right of exit— the right to leave, resign, walk away, become an apostate—which holds for any and all groups, including religious communities (and, in principle at least, the state too).

2. because these groups often don't equip their children with the economic skills they would need to make their way in the world if they did decide to leave; nor have the group's adult members developed within the community the resources that make for a prosperous material existence. The education they provide condemns most of their children to some version of traditionalist poverty or spartan discipline—on the assumption, of course, that this is the good life.

3. because these groups are unlikely to teach their children the values that underlie democratic politics: the equality of citizens, the need for free and open debate, the right of opposition, and, above all, the commitment to a commonweal, or general good, that includes people outside the parochial community—heretics, apostates, infidels, foreigners, and so on.[5]

Assume now that the descriptive statements I have just made are accurate, that totalizing groups behave in these ways. This means that their schools won't, as a matter of principle, produce individuals who are capable of acting autonomously in the world (choosing a career, say, or responding to a calling not ratified by their religion) or capable of reaching for material success; and they won't produce citizens who are ready to take responsibility for the general well-being of a political community that includes "the others." I would even suggest that the reproductive project of totalizing groups depends on these results: the project won't succeed, won't prosper over time, unless new members are taught not to seek autonomy, not to pursue happiness in the form of material welfare, and not to aim at the general, extra-community good. Should the democratic state support, should it even allow, that success?

The first issue raised by this question is the extent of parental rights over children when they are contested not by the children themselves but by other people who claim to have an interest in the future values and behavior of the children. In this case it is the state, or, better, the body of citizens, that claims this interest. I suppose that the usual claim is limited: the citizens have an interest that exists alongside the parental interest and modifies it to such and such a degree. Only if the state were itself a totalizing community, only if it were a totalitarian rather than a liberal state, would it claim a superseding interest.

Let us try to imagine a group of citizens explaining their interest to skeptical or hostile parents. What would they say? They might elaborate on the first and second problematic features of totalizing groups, and urge the right of the children to act autonomously in the world and to pursue (if they so choose) material happiness. Indeed, autonomy is the value liberals most often invoke when they criticize the educational practices of, say, fundamentalist religious communities. But this involves the claim to know what is best for other people's children—a hard claim to defend when what is at issue is the use of state power, and one that I am inclined to bracket and approach only indirectly. An argument focused on the third problematic feature of totalizing communities seems more promising, since now the parents speak for themselves and their own children as citizens and future citizens. But there are still many difficulties, as we will see; the argument that begins here has no end.

The citizens say to the parents, "You may raise your children to be whatever you want them to be, with this qualification: if they are to be citizens, if they are to participate along with our children in the public life of the wider community, to join in debates about domestic and foreign policy, to vote in our elections, then they must be taught something about the history of the country, the meaning of citizenship, and the values of democratic politics. As citizens, they are not simply your children; they are the children of the republic, which means that they are going to make decisions that will determine the shape of our common life, perhaps even the survival of the political community. And they have to be taught their responsibility as citizens so that we can be reasonably confident that they will attend to it. The stakes are high; the decisions they will join in making are of critical importance to all of us."

That is, I think, the minimalist position of the citizens; note that it doesn't specify the extent of the educational role they are claiming. Even if the extent is modest, they will probably have more to say than I have just imagined them saying. The rights of democratic citizenship—free debate, political opposition—overlap with the autonomy rights that I bracketed just a moment ago. Thus, if some of the children of the parochial group claim the right to escape from the discipline of a religious court, say, or from the patriarchal control of group elders, this right (and others, too) will certainly be defended by the officials of the democratic state. "Among us," the officials will say, "all men and women are equal before the law, and this equality must be upheld by the state and enforced by the magistrates, whatever the consequences for particular parochial groups.

Individuals can leave these groups, or become dissidents within them, without any civil penalty—indeed, without costs of any sort so far as the state is concerned."

But this response brings us immediately to the second issue that groups of this sort pose: the extent to which we are prepared to tolerate differences. Liberal advocates of toleration sometimes assume that they are being as tolerant as they can possibly be, as tolerant as anyone could possibly want them to be, when they recognize a very wide range of individual choices. Virtually any imaginable life plan, short of a plan to rob or murder one's fellows, is legitimate, and people can associate freely in support of any plan that requires their cooperation. Many plans, many associations: What more could anyone ask?

In truth, however, the life plans that people form under these conditions of individual freedom turn out (as I suggested in the first chapter) to be remarkably similar to one another. At least, they are similar relative to the range of differences revealed in the historical and anthropological record. People who plan their lives, who make their lives into personal projects, who are entrepreneurs of the self, are one sort among many possible sorts. I know such people intimately, and probably so do most readers of this book. Nonetheless, they have made a rather late appearance in human history; it is only in the past couple of centuries that they have come to dominate Western societies. Today, they are us (or most of us), so we have to ask ourselves: Are we prepared to tolerate men and women for whom autonomy, free choice, and the pursuit of individual happiness are not central values? Are we prepared to tolerate men and women who are differently connected to their own lives—who have inherited rather than chosen their lives, for example, or who bear the yoke of divine command?

Only if we are prepared to tolerate people with lives of that kind can we call ourselves tolerant of *difference*. So, here we are: liberal, democratic citizens. Here they are: members of a total community

that isn't a voluntary association either in fact or in their understanding. What would they say to us when we claim an interest in
their children? "But if you mean to tolerate us," they would say, "if
you mean to recognize our right to live in our own way and to raise
our children to value and sustain that way, then you must allow us
full control over their education. Our way is an integral whole, complete in itself, leaving no aspect of personal or social life without
guidance and constraint. It can't be compromised; it can't be combined with a little bit of this and a little bit of that. Perhaps in the
course of their working lives, many of our sons and daughters will
be forced to move into the larger world and adapt to its manners and
mores. But that makes it all the more important that we control their
education for as long as we can—and it is especially important, critical to our survival, that we control as completely as we can the education and upbringing of our daughters, because it is the daughters who bear the burdens of continuity. They guard the home when
our sons wander; they give to our infant grandchildren their first
words and earliest inclinations.

"In any case, we can't compete for the allegiance of our own
children, for until we have taught them the value of our ways, the
outside world is sure to look more exciting; its materialism is more
enticing than our spartan existence; its gratifications come more
quickly; its responsibilities, for all your talk of citizenship, are much
less onerous than the responsibilities we impose, to God and one
another. We simply can't survive as a voluntary association of autonomous individuals, each one planning his or her own life."

Groups of this sort may or may not be internally democratic
(they are usually dominated by male elders), but they are obviously
hostile to the values of the democratic state whose toleration they
are seeking. Nor is it likely that such a state, or its regime of toleration, would survive if a single totalizing group became demograph-
ically dominant. Nonetheless, there is a strong argument in favor of
tolerating such groups, even in favor of empowering them and pro-

viding some (qualified and conditional) support for their cultural reproduction. This is the argument for multiculturalism, and what it holds is, first, that human beings need the support and nurturing of a cultural community if they are to live decent lives; second, that cultural communities are highly complex entities, created over many generations, with the effort and devotion of many people; third, that men and women don't choose their communities but nonetheless are strongly attached to them, morally and emotionally; and fourth, that the different communities embody values that can't be rank-ordered on a single scale (which doesn't mean that their practices and policies can't be criticized). I shall offer no explicit defense of these four claims, although I was implicitly defending them in my opening discussion of involuntary association . . . and I am doing so here again.

I want to address another dimension of contemporary multiculturalism. The thrust of both recognition and empowerment politics is, in part at least, egalitarian. It should be contrasted with the more standard liberal effort at emancipation: to create autonomous individuals and set them loose and running from their greedy communities. Autonomous individuals are socially mobile; they range up and down the economic ranks, pursuing their opportunities, succeeding or failing in the marketplace. It is important that they be allowed to do that, although we needn't always regard their entrepreneurial activities as liberating or heroic. The communities they leave behind, weak to start with, will only be further weakened by their departure. But some members, many, in fact, won't depart—even when they could "do better" in the larger world. Loyalty to the old ways, as I have already argued, or to specific people and places, will hold them fast. And mutual aid within the community often enables the members to do well enough, reducing the incentive to leave. What would an egalitarian project require then? Should democratic citizens, using the state as their instrument, attempt to lift the group as a whole out of its impoverished or pariah existence—not only by recognizing and respecting its way of life but, if necessary, by subsidizing it?

These questions invite another: Should any group, any way of life, be respected and subsidized without regard to its substantive qualities? Critics of multicultural politics raise the specter of relativism. How can we respect or subsidize totalizing and hierarchical, illiberal and inegalitarian communities? In practice, however, relativism is only a specter; respect and subsidy always have a price, as traditionalist groups discover as soon as they claim their "rights." Rights are liberal constructions; they come with conditions, and so they should. But one of the conditions can't be that the totalizing community transform itself into a standard liberal voluntary association.

It follows that even if the values of the democratic state take precedence over those of the parochial communities *for certain purposes,* those values don't come first in every case. But it isn't easy, even for citizens, to determine the precise extent of legitimate state purposes and of the demands that they can make on community members. The number of purposes is potentially large, but it is disputed at every point: Does the state have an interest in the economic competence of its future citizens? In their understanding of modern science? In their military training? In their acceptance of public health measures? In equal opportunity for their boys and girls? As a political theorist committed to democracy and citizenship, I have a strong inclination to say yes to all those questions. But that can't be the right answer, for it would turn the body of democratic citizens into something much too close to a totalizing community.

Consider for a moment the last of these possible state interests. Should the liberal democratic state require that the children of the parochial community receive an education that provides (or tries to provide) equal autonomy and equal opportunity for boys and girls?[6] Perhaps the question is better put another way: Should the state, for

the sake of equal autonomy and opportunity, take over the education of the community's children? There can't be any doubt that
gender equality as it is understood in contemporary liberal democracies would require a radical takeover. But what happens then to
toleration? And what should we think about the inevitable resistance of the community, its likely withdrawal into deeper poverty
and marginality, and the development among its members of a politics of resentment and paranoia? It may be necessary to choose between dealing with the group's unequal standing in society and
dealing with the unequal standing of its individual members. Liberal political theorists prefer to address the second issue, and that is
an understandable liberal preference. But perhaps the first issue
needs to be addressed . . . first.

That priority would mean looking for ways to move resources
into the community, to help its members generate and collect resources on their own, and to strengthen its welfare and educational
institutions and its life-cycle services—even while it remains a hierarchical community. The anomaly here is that this kind of resource transfer can only be accomplished politically. It requires that
group members participate in the democratic process, defending
their own interests. Consequently, the argument that they have to be
taught the responsibilities that go with participation seems very
strong. Indeed, democratic education should be the crucial condition of any resource transfer—most obviously because a substantial
part of the transferred resources are likely to be spent on schooling.
So the internal hierarchies of group life are tolerated by this version
of egalitarianism but also simultaneously subverted.

Even minimalist state intervention, for the sake of citizenship
rather than autonomy, would challenge the hierarchies of gender
and age. But the challenge would be, as it should be, less than total.
Let's look more closely at the moral and political consequences of
calling group members citizens and encouraging them to participate in the political process.

The democratic state recognizes the legal equality of all its citizens, men and women alike, and grants them the same rights to
vote, hold office, join in campaigns and policy debates, and so on.
The different parochial communities cannot then deny these rights,
as many of them would be inclined to do, to their women members.
Nor are the male elders inclined that way for long; they understand
the value of the vote, and so they want "their" women to go to the
polls. No doubt, they teach the women to defer to their fathers and
husbands in such matters and to vote only as they are told. In fact,
however, the fathers and husbands are taught something very similar: to defer to their elders and vote only for approved candidates.
So the most immediate outcome that totalizing groups produce is
not disenfranchised women but bloc voting of a sort that is alien to
a democratic society.

In well-functioning and well-integrated democracies, group
members routinely disagree, and ought to be able to disagree, about
how to vote. Even in a highly polarized community like contemporary Quebec, the Liberal Party manages to challenge the Nationalists for the support of francophone voters. There is a general truth
here: given a politics of argument and opposition, any claim to
know the one and only right way for members of a community to
respond to its difficulties is sure to be disputed within the community itself. In the United States, for example, if 65 percent of
unionized workers vote Democratic, that is considered a remarkable instance of class discipline. When 85 percent of blacks vote
Democratic, that is taken as a sign of their alienation from the political mainstream. But totalizing groups, when they are politically
mobilized, are likely to deliver even higher percentages of their
votes to a single party or candidate—a sign of more radical alienation. The give-and-take of democratic politics isn't part of the
experience of these voters.

Should it be? Bloc voting is very useful in the politics of resource transfer and therefore in the politics of equality. Still, citi-

zens should know enough about the country in which they live to join the whole range of policy debates—if, when, and as they choose. What can their fellow citizens do to make this possible? Let us imagine citizens collectively claiming a say in the education of all future citizens. This educational project could be accomplished in a variety of ways while leaving the totalizing group in control (but no longer in total control) of its own schools.[7] The state could require that certain secular courses (history, literature, civics) be taught; it could send teachers into the private, parochial, or tribal schools to teach them; it could set examinations that students must pass before being certified as high school graduates; it could take students out of the parochial schools for fixed periods of time, to enroll in national service, perhaps, or simply to show them something of the world outside their own community. Of course, Department of Education officials might do these sorts of things with a heavy hand and with perverse effects. But given some sensitivity and a readiness to negotiate the arrangements in detail, it's not impossible to imagine the officials doing their job well or reasonably well.

Whatever the state did, it would have to do in the same way for boys and girls, and so it would at least open a vista of gender equality. Political participation would do the same with regard to both gender and age, eroding the authority of the male elders. People voting secretly will eventually think about voting differently from the way they are told, and people voting differently, even in secret, will find ways to talk to one another about what they are doing. Still, civic education would not directly challenge the community's way of life. Teachers would focus on the members as citizens, not as autonomous individuals who have to choose beliefs and practices for themselves. Later on, in the course of their political lives, some of these citizens might claim their autonomy rights—more of them, perhaps, the safer their communities are in the larger society. And the state would have to recognize the claims. But it need not anticipate them.

These associations are not voluntary; they are not constituted by the free choices of their individual members. They may or may not move closer to voluntariness; the very existence of a democratic state probably pushes them that way, but every push arouses resistance. In any case, traditionalist and fundamentalist communities are the sites of an intense common life that is, apparently, valued by most of its participants, even if they haven't chosen it. Toleration in a democracy involves acknowledging that evaluation; egalitarianism is well served, I believe, by the same acknowledgment, which its political defenders express by focusing on the group, as well as on the individual members. Again, neither the acknowledgment nor the focus need to be unconditional, but conditions should be coercive only with regard to citizenship, not with regard to individualism. We don't have to, we shouldn't, and we probably can't, force individuals to be free.

Coercion itself cannot be avoided; civic education does have to be legally mandated and compulsory. And since it challenges the totalizing claims of the religious or ethnic community, it is sure to encounter opposition. Its aim is to allow or encourage the community's children, as many of them as possible, to accept another identity, that is, to think of themselves as responsible and respected participants in democratic decisionmaking. Citizens of the state can honestly say that they want these children to *add* citizenship to their existing religious or ethnic self-understanding, not replace the latter with the former. But there is in fact a replacement here: a singular and undivided traditionalism is being replaced by the characteristic dividedness of modern life. If I advocate and pursue that replacement, am I abandoning toleration?

Maybe, but I am not advocating the total replacement of traditional ways. I don't want to insist that members of the parochial or tribal group be taught to draw up their own life plans without copying from their parents. I mean to be more tolerant than contemporary activist versions of liberalism would allow—without, however, endorsing the illiberal way of life of greedy communities. My argument in this chapter moves around and around a dilemma that I can't cut my way through.[8]

It is helpful, however, to think of the dilemma in terms of involuntary association. The groups that I am considering here represent uncommonly strong versions of involuntariness, but involuntariness is not, after all, itself uncommon. It would be an insane political project to try to make it uncommon. Even the liberal state is, for most of its members, an involuntary association. When we set it against the various totalizing communities, that is, set citizens against members, we should be able to recognize the value of compromises worked out between them. But I am still arguing from the side of the citizens. Do the totalizing groups recognize the value of compromise? They don't, of course, and perhaps with good reason, as the parents in my imaginary dialogue explained. Historically, totalizing groups have made their peace with necessary compromises, that is, with arrangements coercively imposed by the state. But they avoid such arrangements whenever they can. And what then? Is it right to compromise with the uncompromising, to tolerate the intolerant?

Here are two legitimate educational projects: in everyday liberal practice, parents have a right to try to sustain a traditional, total way of life, and citizens have a right to educate the young men and women who will soon be responsible for the well-being of the political community. It is the coexistence, the simultaneous legitimacy, of the two rights that makes the difficulty. In other words, democracy makes the difficulty.

Democratic citizenship is an inclusive status (in a way that autonomous individuality isn't), and it is also an official status, a kind of political office that carries with it significant responsibilities. If the members of the total community were not citizens, if their children were not future citizens, there would be no problem. In a multinational or multireligious empire, where all the members of the different nations or religions are imperial subjects whose only responsibility is obedience, the emperor has little reason to interfere in the projects for social reproduction carried on in communal schools. There is no common life for which imperial subjects need to be trained; it is probably in the emperor's interest that no common life emerge. But democracy requires the common life of the public square and the assembly, and certain understandings must be shared among citizens if what goes on in those places is to issue in legitimate laws and policies. Citizens, as Rousseau said, give the law to themselves.[9] But they can't do that if different groups among them are already bound to other, wholly encompassing laws that demand total commitment.

Perhaps these groups, like the Amish in the United States, will agree to live entirely on the margins of the political community, claiming none of the benefits, exercising none of the rights, of citizenship—living as internal exiles within the state.[10] Marginalization is one way of dealing with totalizing groups; if it is successful, they won't be required to give the law to themselves (a good thing, since they believe they already have it), and what is more important, they won't be allowed to give it to citizens outside the group. They will live in a corner of the democratic state as if they were living in a vast empire.

But marginality doesn't solve or even address the inequality problem. And most totalizing groups are inescapably engaged with the larger political community; some, like the ultraorthodox in Israel, are economically dependent on it. They have found a variety of ways to make room for economic dealing, political maneuvering, and prudential decisionmaking, without always acknowledging what they are doing. Hence some sort of negotiation is in fact possible between members and citizens, between parochial groups and the democratic state, even if it is officially disallowed by group elders.

Still, I can't see a principled resolution of the conflict between them—a resolution that each of them *ought* to accept. David Miller, who has written insightfully on these issues, argues that democracy can resolve the conflict, in principle if not always in practice. Imagine a country, he suggests, where all formal education is secular in character. Then "the claim that Islamic schools [are] essential to Muslim identity would have to be assessed on its own merits, and might well be rejected in a democratic forum." To call the rejection illegitimate, Miller argues, is to deny the very essence of citizenship and democracy.[11] Well, maybe. But would the citizens be deciding that Islamic schools were not essential to Muslim survival or that Muslim survival itself was not essential, and how would Muslim parents know which decision their fellow citizens had made? I doubt that the question of Islamic schools can be decided democratically; I am sure that the question of Muslim survival shouldn't be. What the citizens can and must decide is what sort of education, what course of study, is necessary for citizenship. If they are wise, they will set a fairly minimalist standard, even if they hope for more. But whatever they do, they are posing a problem for the members of parochial communities, not resolving a problem.

There just isn't a knockdown answer to the arguments of either citizens or parents: both their projects are justified; neither allows enough room for the other. The liberal democratic state and the greedy community can coexist only in antagonism, for the state demands some significant part of the attention and commitment of the group's members—and the group feels, probably rightly, that any concessions on this point are the beginning of the end. I mean the end of the wholly encompassing way of life, for alternative, more modest or more liberal versions can probably be saved.

There are two other possibilities that I have not yet considered. The first is the collapse of the greedy community, through state-sponsored assimilation, or social pressure from the majority, or the cumulative effects of economic incentives. It has long been thought that the whole tendency of modern social development is in this direction and that coercion would be needed only at the margins. This now looks wrong. In many parts of the world, the conflict between states and totalizing groups is stark, and the use of state power is massive. Some sort of accommodation seems preferable, even if it can't be fully justified to either side.

The other possibility is the collapse of democracy, the takeover of the state or of major state institutions by the totalizing group—empowerment with a vengeance. Again, I am talking here only about the collapse of *liberal* democracy, for some modified version of democratic politics can probably be sustained, as it is in Iran today. Imagine the conflict as a power struggle in which this second possibility is always present. Perfect equilibrium is unlikely; the balance will tilt one way or the other. So the questions that I have been asking can be given a new form: Which way would we tilt the balance if we could?

Now it seems to me that there is a principled position: If political power is at stake, we should tilt decisively against the totalizing groups. Not for the sake of a full-scale liberalism, but for the sake of a minimalist decency. The group's view of others is commonly much harsher than the democratic state's view of group members. The conflict between the two produces ugliness on both sides, but liberal democratic toleration, even if it is finally intolerant of totalizing religions and ethnicities, is gentler, less humiliating, less frightening, than the alternative is likely to be. Liberal democracy has managed to include fundamentalist religions and chauvinist nationalities, as I have been arguing it should, even if it has also modified them in the process, as it also should. Fundamentalism in power and chauvinism with an army are far more likely to exclude than to bring in, and if this is more respectful of difference in that it acknowledges the depth of differences, it has often been far less respectful both of human dignity and of life and limb.

This liberal tilt is simply a guideline for decisionmaking in a political crisis. It doesn't solve the problem of day-to-day coexistence. For that there is no theoretical solution, no deduction from a set of principles, only a long and unstable series of compromises. On the citizens' side, the compromises derive from an acknowledgment of the realities of involuntary association and the values it can produce, and they are driven by hopes for greater equality and easier coexistence. Of course, compromise will make community members unhappy; it will also make citizens unhappy. But universal happiness is not a plausible political project; nor is the pursuit of happiness the necessary subject of political theory.

In the first three chapters I have defended a sociologically sophisticated account of group life, suggested a materialist version of multiculturalism, and argued for a politically complicated response to the claims of illiberal cultures—all these in opposition to the exaggerated individualism of liberal political theory. In the next chapter, I want to reexamine the idea of civil society in the light of these arguments, repeating some things I said in my critique of the bad utopia of free association. But civil society figures so largely in political literature these days that the repetition is excusable. And even if the standard liberal account of civil society is utopian in the way I have criticized, it is also descriptive: it claims to be a picture of the world we live in, which opens it to sociological correction. We need to engage with the realities of our own civil society—not only with the freedom it sometimes embodies but also with the hierarchies it sustains. And then we need to revise the liberal account.

FOUR

Civil Society and the State

IVIL SOCIETY IS A DESCRIPTIVE TERM, A
sociological construction, and a liberal dream.
The dream is spun out of the theory of voluntary association: it evokes a world that includes
all the social groups where membership is freely
chosen and non-coercive—and only those. The
family, whose members are not volunteers, is left out, and so is the
state, which, even if its legitimacy rests on the consent of its members, wields coercive power over them.[1] Between these two, autonomous individuals form a multitude of associations and move
freely from one group to another or from core activism to peripheral passivity, and back again. That is the dream. They are moti-
vated by interest or conviction or by cultural or religious identity;
they pursue wealth (in partnerships and companies), or political
power (in parties and movements), or salvation (in churches and
gathered congregations); or they aim to advance some particular

good (in interest groups or trade unions), or to deliver some general benefit (in philanthropies and foundations), or to ward off some evil (in organizations for the prevention of this or that). Civil society makes room for all these aims and includes all the resulting associations by virtue of their free and consensual character. This means that it reaches to politics and economics as well as to the multitude of social activities distinct from those two.

There are theorists who would exclude whatever goes on in the marketplace and sometimes also in the political arena from their account of civil society, perhaps because they don't think of such goings-on as "civil." I see no good reason for the exclusion and have adopted an extended definition. If unions, for example, are included, as they commonly are, then why not the companies with which they are engaged in negotiations over money and job security? To be sure, giant corporations often exercise statelike and near-coercive powers. But their "members," workers as well as stockholders and managers, come and go; they are free agents, not only in principle but to some degree in practice, too.[2] Any realistic description of associational life, whatever groups it includes or leaves out, will have to qualify the idea of free agency: we are all free to some degree.

Even the extended definition isn't extended enough to account for our associational life as it really is—or to explain its hierarchical structures. The enduring inequalities of contemporary society, as I have been arguing, mark off groups that aren't usefully described, even with qualification, as free and consensual, and the ranks and orders within and among these groups are never deliberated or agreed on. Of course, associations for the advancement of some racial or religious interest, or for collective self-defense, or for a particular form of cultural expression will be included in standard liberal accounts of civil society, since their members must join up; no one is born a member of the NAACP or the Anti-Defamation League or the National Organization of Women. It seems to me,

however, that civil society also includes the more inchoate groupings that these associations claim to represent, into which people are
indeed born, which they leave only with difficulty (if at all), and
which many of them would acknowledge if asked to "identify themselves." These groupings provide the necessary background of all
associational activity and give to that activity its (relative) coherence
and stability.

Civil society isn't, then, a free and indeterminate intermingling
of individuals; its shape depends on the pattern of givenness that I
described in Chapter 1. Race, religion, and gender are right now the
most crucial features of that pattern in its American version, providing reference points for the contemporary politics of recognition
and empowerment. This politics has to be worked out within the associational world of civil society. But the working out will require us
to give up the dream of a perfect voluntarism. It will also require a
little help from the state.

As conceived in liberal theory, all the groups that constitute civil
society occupy a common terrain across which individuals move
freely. Because of this freedom, many men and women are members
of different associations, often of many different associations. In
their readiness to "join up," they are not monogamists, not even serial monogamists; they are serial pluralists. This pluralism is crucial
to the attractiveness of civil society. Multiple and overlapping memberships make for peaceful, even if highly contentious, coexistence;
they tie all the groups (or, perhaps better, all their individual members) together, creating something larger and more encompassing
than any of them. This larger entity is still a particular grouping,
namely, the civil society of a country, defined (but not absolutely) by
its political boundaries. Some groups extend across those boundaries, like the Catholic church, or the Socialist International, or new
social movements like environmentalism and feminism, but these
are likely to have local branches that take on the characteristics of a

particular civil society. Irish and French Catholics, say, are characteristically different from each other, as are French and German socialists. Voluntary (and involuntary) association takes place mostly among the members of a political community.

If there were a Sartrean "series" of groups, an unlinked set of associations, without overlap, without any coming and going, without movement of members from one group to another, with minimal conversation across the boundaries, we wouldn't call this a civil society.[3] And if there were a rule, even an implicit and unenforceable rule, that each person belonged to only one association or one set of associations—because of his or her social class, say, or because of religious or racial or gender identity—the resulting society would not be civil in the liberal sense. Membership would be a trap, even if it were still, formally, a choice. It's not that this serial society would be a simple aggregation: so many class organizations and faith communities, say, with no connections of any sort among them. More likely, exclusive memberships would breed intense forms of hostility, so that "civility" either wouldn't exist or would always be at risk.

Civil society does include intolerant and illiberal associations—the greedy or totalizing groups that I have already discussed. They do not dominate the associational world, but they are significant within it. And they organize their common life against the background of the more inchoate groupings, unchosen and categorical, which commonly determine not only identity but social status, too, and which don't encourage comings and goings. A sociologically sophisticated and politically useful account of civil society must somehow encompass all this, even if the groups and groupings are, as they often are, enemies of freedom and pluralism.[4]

Of course, individuals are entitled to devote all their time and energy to a single group if they are so inclined, and many of them do, even choosing groups that don't demand that kind of devotion. But in an open society, without rigid class hierarchies or systematic racial, religious, or sexual segregation, most people won't do that. Historically, it seems fair to say, liberalism has made for plurality and for divided time and energy. Yet neither the exclusive groups nor the inchoate and categorical groupings have disappeared, as liberal theorists expected them to do. Race, religion, ethnicity, class, and gender—all these continue to give rise to identities and institutions that manage to sustain themselves, sometimes on the margins, sometimes in the very center of civil society.

But aren't the values of liberalism antithetical to everything that is categorical, unchosen, and exclusive? And, given the freedom of civil society, won't these values have an effect over time, eroding primordial loyalties and undermining greedy groups? Who would not choose freely and often, given the chance? And how can choice of that sort possibly reproduce the inherited tribalisms of contemporary civil society? Perhaps it is only the time frame of liberal expectation that needs revision.

Consider how liberal values might work their way, not soon, but steadily over decades or centuries. Civil society is, again, a realm of free choice and voluntary participation.[5] The first of these is sometimes said to be unimaginable in its absence. In fact, I can easily imagine individuals choosing spouses, say, and also jobs or professions, in a world with little or no associational pluralism. A more generalized version of free choice would not be available, however; and the generalized version is very attractive. Civil society makes it possible to choose not only among possible individual lives but also among patterns of economic cooperation, among political ideologies and religious faiths, and among complex "forms of life"—and then to keep on choosing. Within civil society, individuals can join or leave a great variety of groups. Within these groups, they can establish stronger or weaker ties with fellow members and devote more or less time and energy to everyday organizational work, internal debates, collective celebrations, committee meetings, social gatherings, and so on. Surely the experience of choosing among all these possibilities will gradually undermine the old ties of birth and blood and the constraining customs of religious and ethnic communities. Even if, right now, only some individuals make these choices, won't their lives seem more interesting to the sedentary, cautious, or repressed others? Won't their number grow?

A more perfect civil society requires interesting men and women, eager to choose, and free to choose, among their many alternatives, but it also requires men and women ready to tolerate the choices of the others—or else the others won't be free for long. So I need to tell a more elaborate story of how liberal values triumph in the associational world. And then I will need to explain why this triumph is likely to be radically incomplete even over the long run.

Democratic citizenship should be part of this story of free choice, voluntary participation, and mutual toleration. As members of the political community, citizens are invited to join with their fellows in the common and contentious work of giving the law to themselves. And some of them do join, engaging themselves locally or nationally on behalf of some set of political interests or beliefs. But what Aristotle called the "friendship" of citizens is attenuated in the modern state, and for most of the citizen-friends, participation is reduced to the bare minimum of voting at election time. State agencies and assemblies rarely play a central role in their everyday life (unless they are soldiers or bureaucrats or politicians). The actual experience of freely chosen solidarities, willing cooperation with other people, and the acquisition of the different kinds of competence associated with cooperative work—these take place largely in the groups that make up civil society.

Political theorists sometimes describe these groups as schools for citizens, as if their value were only preparatory and instrumental.[6] They can indeed serve as schools, and most studies of political participation suggest that there is a link between engagement in state politics, on the one hand, and in civil society, on the other, although the causal direction of the link is uncertain. Active men and women tend to be active everywhere.[7] But it is probably also true for most of them that their most satisfying engagements, where they are most likely to work closely with other people, achieve something they value, and recognize themselves in the achievement, take place in their churches, unions, movements, or mutual aid organizations— in civil society, that is, and not in the state.

These engagements bring people into conflict with one another, exactly as partisan engagement in state agencies and assemblies does. But the intensities are greater in civil society, which is a realm of difference and fragmentation and therefore a realm of conflict, a realm of competing causes, interest groups, companies, parties, even churches and philanthropies. The competition is sometimes for power and influence, sometimes for money, sometimes for members; sometimes it reflects programmatic disagreement, sometimes only personal rivalry. But there is no avoiding it, and it may well be that the most important thing people learn in civil society is how to live with the many different forms of social conflict.[8]

The living is easier if there isn't a single, dominant, all-encompassing conflict between exclusive groups—and that is probably a necessary condition for the existence of both liberal politics and civil society. Under ordinary conditions of competition and counter-vailing power, what participants experience is sometimes painful, sometimes exhilarating, and often tedious and dull—victory or defeat, usually on a small scale, and the long days in between, and then victory or defeat again, for contention is permanent and no outcome is final. But there are many conflicts and, again, liberal expectation hangs on the experience of pluralism. The same people are differently involved in this conflict and that one, and ideally no one is always triumphant or always defeated. Even if the protagonists begin with some religious or political vision of a fully coherent civil society, populated only by people like themselves, most of them come slowly to recognize that the purposes they support, the beliefs they hold, are not and never will be universally supported or held. They are forced to reckon with, and perhaps eventually to understand, the opposition of others (but the others are not always the same people).

Civil society is a school indeed—for competitive coexistence and toleration, which is to say, for civility. At the same time, it is a school for hostility and sometimes for zeal, but these latter passions work to shut down civil society, and insofar as they fail in this aim, their protagonists find that they have no choice but to live with men and women who disagree with them but whom they cannot either eliminate or subjugate. Gradually, the totalizing ideologies and the singular identities give way to a politics of accommodation, even to some (limited) degree of mutual recognition, which in turn opens opportunities for individual engagements across group boundaries. Toleration for the free choices of the others wins out in the end, if only because of the exhaustion of its enemies.

So liberal values will slowly come to govern the practices of civil society. Involuntary associations will never disappear; greedy groups will continue to make their claims; but civil society won't come under their thumb. It will be a home for the protagonists of freedom and pluralism: for their cooperative projects, their engagements and disengagements, and their conflicts. What was utopian at the beginning will become, and ought to become, everyday reality.

But this too is a dream. Freedom and pluralism are indeed worth fighting for, but their achievement is far more complicated than liberal voluntarism suggests. They are continually threatened by the deep inequalities of existing civil society.

The process of developing liberal values is not self-starting or self-sustaining. Civil society cannot become a home for either freedom or pluralism without state action. The exhaustion that makes for tolerance, to take the easiest example, depends today on the democratic state (as it once depended on the absolutist state), which has to hold the ring and make sure that conflicts within civil society never end with the radical subordination of any of the participants and that the norms of civility, at least in some minimalist version, are maintained. By itself, however, holding the ring isn't enough. Even if the victory of some dominant group isn't absolute and permanent, since the struggle against it can always be renewed, reiterated victory by the same group is also dangerous to liberal values. And reiterated victory is a better definition of dominance and a more accurate description of what actually happens in the social world. By contrast, pluralism depends on a rough equality among at least some of the contending groups (or coalitions of groups)—in the sense that we say of teams in major league baseball that, on any given day, any one of them can defeat any other. Not only is it necessary that different groups or coalitions are involved in the ongoing struggles; it is also necessary that more than one of them is realistically in contention for victory. And because only the state can guarantee that no group or coalition is permanently excluded from realistic contention, state officials can't simply hold the ring; they have to intervene on behalf of the weakest groups.

Most of the time, however, they don't do that. Most of the time, the state is, as Marx argued, the ruling committee of the strongest groups. Civil society is not a genuinely pluralist realm; it is something less than that. Or something nastier: some members of both dominant and excluded groups are likely to drift toward a xenophobic politics and to form very ugly associations. The logic of mutual accommodation depends on pluralism working in a roughly egalitarian way.[9]

Similarly, any effective version of individual freedom requires a significant degree of equality within the different groups, among the members. But many of the groups included in a pluralist civil society are organized hierarchically; many of them actively enforce inequality, crucially between men and women, also between old and young. These inequalities are a feature not only of some dominant groups but also of some weak and marginal ones, where we might expect a more egalitarian disposition to arise. Especially in traditionalist religious and ethnic communities, the freedom and mobility of subordinate members, women most importantly, are radically curtailed. The state could act on behalf of these subordinate members, but most of the time it supports the dominant elites. When that happens, civil society is not a realm of freedom.

If the dream of civil society were our waking state, if voluntarism were the true and effective principle of associational life, both the external and the internal inequalities that I have just described would never arise. In the perfect civil society of our promised future (which would be something like a perfect market), there would be no inferior groups or individuals, no curtailments of opportunity or denials of rights—for men and women would simply not join, or would quickly leave, associations in which or because of which they were systematically subordinated. Women would walk away from the Catholic church, from Islam, from orthodox Judaism, and from any tribal or aboriginal collective in which they were denied equal opportunity; Jews would assimilate into the local mainstream (whatever it was); blacks would pass (if they could), and so on. The list of potential escapes is very long, and the associational world would certainly look different if all of them were accomplished; it would be less conflict-ridden and far less diverse. There might still be many associations, but they would all look very much the same. The state would have no work to do in civil society. Should this be our goal—to make state action permanently unnecessary? Here, again, is the utopia of voluntary association and individual mobility. The more that men and women are free to move and the more groups there are to which they can escape, the more difficult it is to maintain either subjection or hierarchy.

I have been arguing all along that this perfect civil society is an impossible dream. The inevitable background of involuntary association, the necessary socialization of children, the loyalty or inertia of members—all these explain the impossibility. Still, liberal theorists find it hard to set the dream aside. Perhaps we should make free choice and radical mobility a regulative idea. Perhaps we should work steadily toward, even if we know we can never reach, a civil society in which the inequalities of associational life would finally be abolished, in which all individuals would be emancipated and no groups would be empowered, or would need to be. To begin with, we might make it as easy as we can, in the social world as we know it, for individuals to shift from one group to another. Shouldn't this be our goal? Why in the world not?

These are classic "exit, voice, and loyalty" questions, and I will very briefly restate the answer suggested by Albert Hirschman in his book of that name.[10] The most vigorous and independent people are certain to exit first, and in the groups they leave behind, the voices of dissent and protest, and the capacity for internal reform, will be radically diminished. People who can't or won't make their escape—and there will be a lot of them—will find themselves in a significantly weaker position. That's why loyalty has to be a central value of any decent associational life. We can imagine an almost absolute freedom, like that claimed by the seventeenth-century English radical Robert Everard when he told Oliver Cromwell that "whatsoever hopes or obligations I should be bound unto, if afterwards God should reveal himself, I would break it speedily, if it were a hundred a day." But we cannot imagine an attractive set of associations inhabited and sustained by people like Everard. Cromwell's response seems entirely justified: engagements should not be broken whenever someone imagines his personal scruples to be warnings from God.[11] When we educate our children to be members of some particular group or association, we commonly mean to teach them a stronger loyalty than Everard recognizes—not only so that the group will survive over time but also so that it can be reformed from within. And this is true even if we acknowledge the plurality of groups to which we belong and the (different) plurality to which our children will belong. We want them to understand the burdens of membership as well as the right of withdrawal.

In fact, this understanding is widely shared, which is, again, one important reason why the social world cannot be explained as the work of autonomous individuals and why there will never be a perfect civil society (any more than there will ever be a perfect market). Voluntary associations coexist with involuntary ones; men and women who have chosen to be where they are stand alongside men and women who have remained where they found themselves. Despite the attractions of free choice and the excitements of coming and going, the appeal of membership and belonging, of tradition and habit, even of inequality and authority, is very strong. Liberal political theorists have only begun to understand it.

Because of the existing, often illiberal and hierarchical "givenness" of civil society, whatever version of freedom and pluralism is possible can only be a *political* achievement; it will not be achieved by individuals acting alone, or even voluntarily cooperating, over however long a period of time. And this politics can be undertaken and advanced through only one agency. Among groups and within them, at the top of the status hierarchy and at the bottom, state action is necessary if civil society is to work.

But this state action has to take a complicated form, for freedom and pluralism sometimes come into conflict with each other. The inclusiveness of pluralism extends to groups that are not sympathetic to liberal conceptions of freedom. At the same time, the commitment to freedom raises questions precisely about this pluralist extension. The liberal state presides over a social union of social unions that incorporates and even protects illiberal associations. Faced with this apparent contradiction, the standard liberal response has been to minimize the role of the state, insisting upon its neutrality, refusing to distinguish among the many different associations, allowing them all to flourish if they can—on the assumption that they will flourish only if they satisfy the needs and aspirations of their members.[12] More recently, under pressure from feminist writers (who rightly deny the assumption), some liberal theorists have expanded the state's role, so that liberalism becomes something like a totalizing ideology, aimed at the universal establishment of individual autonomy and associational freedom.[13] Each of these views emphasizes only one of the values of civil society. The point, it seems to me, is to hold the two, freedom and pluralism, in balance. It is necessary to bring the state in—but only so far.

Consider first the hierarchy of groups. Whether or not it includes market associations, civil society reflects group inequality and, if left to its own devices, is likely to reinforce and augment its effects. This is so because every organized group is also a mobilization of resources: the more resources its members bring with them, the stronger the group. The stronger the group, the more able it is to enhance the impact of the resources it collects. Hence it is a general rule of civil society that its strongest members get stronger.[14] Either the weaker and poorer members are unable to organize at all—they are excluded or marginalized—or they form groups that reflect their weakness and poverty. Of course, these groups can also serve, to some degree, to make their members less weak and poor. Numbers are a potent resource in a democracy, and civil society provides space for mass mobilizations that, in certain historical junctures, can reshape the established hierarchies of wealth and power. But these mobilizations are rare, in part because they are likely to require, before they can succeed, the assistance of the democratic state (as the American labor movement required the Wagner Act and the National Labor Relations Board).

In the absence of such assistance, the greatest danger of civil society is often realized: exclusion from it. The benefits of association are captured by those citizens who already possess the time and money necessary to form strong organizations and the education and skill necessary to run them effectively. Sometimes, when this happens, impoverished citizens and members of stigmatized groups are simply reduced to anonymity and silence; they become invisible men and women, and the pluralism of civil society is radically curtailed. But another outcome is possible because of the self-consciously multicultural character of contemporary civil society, where the crucial divisions reflect not only class difference but also racial, religious, and gender difference, and where these two partly coincide. This is the politics of identity and recognition, which I take to be (though it need not be) the politics of civil society's dispossessed.[15] It is, as I have already argued, an egalitarian politics, though not a politics effective enough in serving its ends.

Men and women who cannot mobilize resources for a successful defense of their interests or for a satisfying enactment of their cultural values live not only with a sense of deprivation but also with a sense of disrespect. We commonly think of status and reputation as attributes of individuals, perhaps also of families, and we imagine conflict in civil society as having some larger purpose, material or ideological in character. But when the members of excluded or marginalized groups are oppressed because of their membership, their standing in the world is a collective, not an individual, issue: they stand or fall together. Their collective condition might suggest the need for redistributive policies aimed at providing resources and opportunities to individuals—to liberate them from identities or, at least, from conditions that they have not chosen (this is the emancipation option). But, for very good moral and psychological reasons, collective deprivation also leads to a political defense of the devalued identities, articulated in a demand for respect: an acting out, with a plural pronoun, of the old American insistence on equality: "Call me mister!"[16]

Identity politics is only sometimes aimed directly at the state— as when a subordinated group with an established territorial base demands autonomy or secession. When groups are dispersed, as they commonly are in immigrant societies and, increasingly, in nation-states, the acting out of the demand for respect takes place mostly in civil society—most importantly in schools, but since I have already discussed the education of members and citizens, I will focus now on associational life more generally. Identity politics greatly intensifies the normal conflicts of civil society, for it makes racial, religious, and gender difference an issue at every point where it is experienced, in everyday encounters and conversations, in the competition of groups, in the self-government and internal life of associations. Hate speech and "political correctness" are controversial chiefly in civil society even when the state is asked to deal with them. I doubt that anyone has been collecting statistics about this, but I would guess that questions of group representation arise at least as often in civil associations as in the civil service of the state, and probably in ways that involve more people. The demand for public acknowledgment of the existence, achievements, and needs of minority groups is probably made more often in companies, unions, churches, parties, philanthropic organizations, professional associations, and so on, than in more official settings. Men and women search for ways to take pride in who they are more often as workers or believers or neighbors than as citizens. The pathologies of the search are experienced more often as distortions of everyday life than as distortions of citizenship; the benefits, if and when they come, are associational more than political.

The problems of inequality have to be dealt with in civil society, which is a realm of inequality. How can this be done? Two different responses to this question have emerged in recent debates. The first is the work of neoconservative intellectuals, but it reflects a near-classical liberalism. It holds that "we" shouldn't do anything; individual men and women must take responsibility for their own lives—not only individually but also in (voluntary) association, pooling resources, bringing their numbers to bear, acting on their own behalf. The associational life of civil society is, on this view, self-correcting. And even if the corrections take a long time, the work that they require is morally, maybe also spiritually, uplifting; it builds character. So we should simply step back and not interfere with the self-interested activity of men and women freely forming and reforming the organizations that they need.[17]

The second argument is egalitarian or social democratic. Its protagonists commonly call for state action, as I have been doing. On this view, the state should aim first at providing encouragement and support for those needed organizations, so that they are actually organized, which they often won't be without external assistance. It should aim second at responding to the demands the organizations are sure to make for a redistribution of resources—whether directly through the tax system or through education, job training, reverse discrimination, welfare entitlements, and so on.

There is a sense, perhaps, in which both these views are right, but only if they are taken together. State action cannot replace the spontaneous workings of civil society, but civil society won't work without state action. The distribution of responsibility is, as we used to say, dialectical.

We can think better about how the dialectic works if we consider the economic base of civil society. Thus far, I have described associations as mobilizing the resources of their members. That is an accurate description, but it misses a great deal; it misses, in the American case, half or more of the money that is dispensed by many associations. This money comes from the state, but it comes in a great variety of ways, often in disguise. It comes, for example, in the form of tax exemptions for philanthropic gifts and nonprofit organizations (exemptions that leave no record in the budgets of the organizations that spend the money, although without them there would be far less money to spend). It comes in the form of subsidies and subventions, matching grants and low-interest loans, services provided by the state (including regulatory services), and entitlements paid by the state on behalf of individuals to privately run health and welfare services (often organized by religious communities).[18] In a famous speech, the first President Bush spoke of voluntary associations as "points of light" in American society, as if government, by contrast, was a realm of darkness. In fact, there would be very little light if the state did not organize and maintain the electrical networks and subsidize the costs of energy.

In principle, this state funding ought to have equalizing effects on civil society, but it will have these effects only if they are part of its design. The inequalities of associational life are also inequalities of political power and competence and therefore of access to tax money. Some people in some groups know better than others how to get the money—partly because of the people they know, the networks in which they are located, and partly because of the things they know about how the system works. So it isn't enough simply to tell people to organize and go to work, although that is no doubt a good thing to tell them. It is also necessary to make sure that the assistance the state provides to associational life is directed first of all to the weakest associations.

I have already argued that if these associations, which are largely those of minority groups, were significantly strengthened and enabled to provide cultural and welfare services for their members, the pathologies of identity politics (resentment, hatred, narrow chauvinism) would mostly disappear, resurfacing now and again only on the political margins. A strong associational life is an achievement in which people will take pride and which will command respect in the larger world, even if it requires state help (everyone gets state help, after all). But this isn't yet a program, only a hope; state help comes to those who demand it, effective demand requires organization, and some groups are more capable than others of organizing themselves. To announce a principle of egalitarian assistance—to help the weakest groups first—is much less difficult than to describe the process through which this principle might be realized. What is most immediately necessary is to provide legal support and professional counsel to those groups whose demands are not currently effective.

I do not think that every organization of the weak should be subsidized or assisted by the liberal state. I will consider the problems posed by illiberal groups later on. Claims on tax money collected from the citizens of a democracy have to be defended in front of the citizens, so the organizations making the claims must be "citizenly," at least in a minimal sense.

State and civil society resemble the chicken and the egg. No significant move toward greater equality has ever been made without state action, but states don't act in egalitarian ways unless they are pressed to do so by mobilizations that can take place only in civil society—and that already represent a move toward greater equality. The mobilization of black Baptists in the American civil rights movement of the early 1960s is a useful example. If we were to tell that story, looking for some pattern of causation the way historians do, where would we begin? With Supreme Court decisions and presidential orders or with bus boycotts and student sit-ins? In Washington, D.C., Montgomery, Alabama, or Raleigh, North Carolina? In a lawyer's office or a church basement? Even after the fact, we cannot easily assign causal responsibility, let alone know in advance where to start a move toward greater equality.

The politics of civil society is necessarily experimental. And one of the things that we have learned from this particular American experiment is that the achievement of civil rights, by itself, isn't enough. Without a redistribution of resources and an empowerment of groups, the emancipation of black Americans (the end of legal segregation and discrimination) amounted to only one step toward equality when two steps were necessary. If those black Baptist churches were running day-care centers, hospitals, old-age homes, and family-assistance programs with resources equivalent to those of white Lutherans, Presbyterians, and Jews, everyday life in the United States would look different than it does. I can't gauge the difference: small, perhaps, but very important. This is the meat-and-potatoes multiculturalism that I argued for in Chapter 2: civil society is its proper location.[19]

Even without radical freedom and mobility, everything in civil society, in principle and often enough in practice, is subject to revision. But no one is in charge of the revisions. Any entrepreneur, ideologist, or prophet, any man or woman with a project, can try to form an association. On the liberal understanding, all associations are self-organizing (although the state may sometimes regulate the process, as it does with corporations and labor unions). In the absence of political or military coercion, groups spontaneously appear and disappear. But there is at any given moment an existing civil society, even if it is changing as we watch; and men and women committed to equality have to figure out how to relate to this associational world—which is sure to include illiberal and nonegalitarian groups.

Religious believers and political militants tend to pose the question differently: How would we organize civil society if we had the chance? Or, what would civil society look like if everyone shared our faith or ideology? Those can't be my questions here; they aren't liberal questions. I assume a civil society that already includes the Atheists' Association, the Rosicrucians, Masonic lodges, the Trotskyists, the California Monarchist Society, General Motors, the National Organization of Women, B'nai B'rith, the Animal Rights League, Pentecostal sects, the Amish, the United Auto Workers, the Catholic church, the Elks and the Lions, the Nation of Islam, the Jews, black and Chinese and Hispanic collectives, and so on and on and on. This is what John Rawls calls the "fact of pluralism," and this fact extends to cultural and moral as well as organizational diversity.[20] We commonly encounter groups that reject the deepest values of the liberal democratic state that frames and protects them, and that also reject the values of the wide-ranging and disorganized civil society in which they find a place.

In theory, civil society is created by autonomous individuals, but in practice many of its associations are unfriendly to autonomy. More than this, many of the groups that coexist in civil society, that seek recognition and empowerment within it, are not themselves liberal or democratic, even though they appeal to liberal and democratic norms. Let's consider now the inequalities that prevail within them, in the form of charismatic leadership, hierarchical organization, elite dominance, and gender discrimination. The effect of all these, singularly or together, is that some of the members are more free than others. If we are concerned about freedom, the question we have to ask is not, How do we express this value?—as if we could just walk around in civil society expressing it. The question is, How do we defend freedom under conditions, first, of group autonomy and, second, of hierarchical subordination in many of the autonomous groups? Or, given the fact of pluralism, what sorts of subordination and what sorts of subordinating practices are we prepared to tolerate, and what sorts not, in the civil society of a democratic state?[21]

Answering these questions isn't easy; nor is there one answer for all occasions and all associations. We require democratic elections in labor unions, for example, but not in churches. I suppose that there are good reasons for this difference—which have to do with our ideas about religious freedom, with the relative oldness of churches and newness of unions, and with the role of the state in union organization. On the other hand, we have barred polygamy among the Mormons, although it is an old practice, justified in religious terms.

The argument that I sketched in my discussion of fundamentalist religions and other greedy or totalizing groups distinguished the problematics of society and politics: first, there are associational practices that radically curtail the life chances of members, and, second, there are practices that limit the rights or deny the responsibilities of citizenship. The harder problems are posed by the first. What constitutes radical curtailment? More fundamentally, what range of life chances is required by the idea of individual autonomy? There is no single necessary list for all times and places. Nor is it clear that autonomy in a given time and place requires equal access to every locally available life chance. In fact, many sorts of restrictions are compatible with the existence, even the flourishing, of autonomous individuals, however undesirable they are from the standpoint of liberal theory. But which sorts of restrictions?

It turns out to be much easier to adopt the criteria suggested by the second, political problematic, which has to do with the rights and responsibilities of citizens. What is at issue, after all, is not social criticism but state intervention, and liberal democratic states may do better if they avoid philosophical disputes about the meaning of autonomy and instead focus on the requirements of citizenship. The policy of the Catholic church that bars the priesthood to women, for example, even though it will be opposed by liberal egalitarians, doesn't qualify on these grounds as a reason for state intervention: no one has a right to be a priest, nor do citizens need to have access to the priesthood in order to function well in democratic politics. But a refusal to educate Catholic (or Hasidic or Amish or Native American) women, or any radical curtailment of their education, would qualify, not only because it limits their life chances but also because it denies them the skills and knowledge that we judge to be necessary for all citizens. The case is the same with practices that deny women fair access to family resources or control over the schedule of their daily activity. Both of these are necessary to effective political participation. It may not be possible or prudent to ban practices like these, but organizations and groups within which such practices exist can legitimately be denied state subsidy and support. When faith-based or ethnically based groups, for example, provide welfare services with tax money, the services can rightly be constrained by some set of egalitarian principles (but we can argue about the dimensions of the set).

This is the proposal that I have already made and defended: in working out state policy, we don't have to refer to individual autonomy but only to the mutual dependency of democratic citizens. This proposal is both an argument for and a qualification of my opening claim, that civil society requires a strong state. Since the defense of that claim starts from the non-state associations that people find themselves in, or join, or create, and acknowledges the value of these associations, it isn't a statist argument. Still, it serves to distinguish my own social democratic commitments from standard liberalism, which has its origin in a rebellion not only against organized religion but also against organized politics. Liberals have always insisted that autonomous individuals need to be protected against the power of state officials; they are less solicitous of autonomous groups that don't value individualism. Social democrats, by contrast, although we accept the need for constitutional limits on what state officials can do, are ready at the same time to recognize the usefulness of their power and to give them room to exercise it. But we are more willing, or ought to be, to shield the solidarities of collective life.[22] These, then, are the central propositions of a social democratic theory of civil society:

1. Civil society in the real world is not just a collection of voluntary associations; its overall character is not determined by individual comings and goings.

2. Because of what else there is besides voluntarism and mobility, civil society cannot work as liberals want it to work without the help of the state.

3. The state must act not only to regulate the conflicts that arise within civil society but also to remedy the inequalities produced by the strengths and weaknesses of the different groups and by their internal hierarchical arrangements.

4. When the state intervenes in civil society, it cannot aim to reproduce its liberalism in all the associations; it acts sometimes for political freedom, sometimes for associational pluralism, and only sometimes for both together.

At certain historical moments, civility and association stand in radical opposition to the state. The classic example is Eastern Europe in the last years of communist rule, when intellectuals and activists launched the late-twentieth-century revival of the civil society argument. Radical opposition, however, is a difficult position to generalize. In a tyrannical state, the terrain of civility is narrowly circumscribed and the mobility of individuals is constrained. Civil society takes on a romantic character. Life within it is rather like an underground activity; its oppositional values lead to a voluntary repression of internal conflicts, generating fierce loyalties and utopian aspirations—above all, the aspiration for the replacement of the state by pure associationalism. George Konrad's "antipolitics," a response to the communist restoration in Hungary after the failed revolution of 1956, is a useful and attractive illustration.[23] But antipolitics in practice would quickly generate all the usual inequalities of civil society. So the collapse of the unfriendly state reveals the need for a friendly state, that is, for regulation, redistribution, and (sometimes) intervention.

Since we can never construct a perfect civil society, the state will never, not even in the best of times, be the "night watchman" that classical liberalism envisaged (and it will never "wither away," as Marxists expected). Nor will its commitments to individualism and autonomy ever be as pervasive in our associational life as today's activist liberals would like. In its relation to civil society, the friendly state defends equality while holding pluralism and freedom in balance.

But this friendliness can never be guaranteed. Regulation, redistribution, and intervention invite abuse; even states that have foresworn totalitarian ambition are still power-driven and (often) corrupt. As there is no perfectly self-sufficient civil society, so there is no perfectly serviceable state. The members of civil society must also be committed and vigilant citizens. It is one of the less recognized truths of egalitarian politics that sometimes, when minority groups come into conflict with the state, equality is best served if the state wins. This is sometimes the case with totalizing and also with hierarchical associations. Equality, however, requires other, more familiar victories: over tyrannical state officials, over corporate power, over ancient wealth and privilege, and over the entrenched strength of dominant groups. The commitment and vigilance of citizens is necessary in all these cases. State action for equality requires the democratic mobilization of larger numbers of citizens than any of the groups include. It requires cross-group social movements; sometimes it requires an insurrectionary politics.

The next two chapters examine some neglected aspects of movements and insurrections and of democratic politics generally, beginning with what is left out of the liberal picture of autonomous individuals deliberating about what ought to be done. This picture is attractive, in much the same way that civil society is attractive, but it is also utopian, ignoring the demands of social conflict and reflecting a certain dislike for the all-too-human intensities of democratic politics. I will argue that democracy and equality require a more material engagement.

FIVE

Deliberation . . . and What Else?

ELIBERATIVE DEMOCRACY IS THE AMERI-can version of German theories of commu-nicative action and ideal speech. Characteristi-cally, it exists at a lower level of philosophical development and justification—which makes it more accessible to people like me, who live at that lower level—and its defenders turn more readily than German philosophers do to questions of public policy and institutional arrangements. They are not focused on the rationally ascertainable presuppositions of human discourse but rather on the practical or-ganization and likely outcomes of normatively constrained political arguments. The presuppositions are presupposed, without any elaborate demonstration of their philosophical standing.

Still, deliberative democracy is emphatically a *theory* about pol-itics, and it represents an interesting development of American lib-eralism—a shift from a discourse of rights to a discourse of decision. To be sure, the second of these looks back to the first, retaining, as I shall argue, a certain bias for the courtroom. Nonetheless, the recent outpouring of books and articles about deliberative democracy is impressive, and many of the arguments are persuasive.

There hasn't been enough disagreement about deliberation in the United States, however, and there has been hardly any effort at all to consider its contexts and necessary complements; the idea is already in danger of becoming a commonplace.[1] So I intend to indulge a contrarian impulse and list the nondeliberative activities that democratic politics legitimately, perhaps necessarily, involves. I doubt that the list is exhaustive, although I haven't knowingly left anything out. As will quickly become obvious, I have not made deliberation synonymous with thinking; the activities that I want to describe are not thoughtless or ill-considered. But they are not deliberative in the ideal or programmatic sense intended by theorists of deliberative democracy, either; that is, they are not aimed at reaching decisions through a rational process of discussion among equals, who listen respectfully to each other's views, weigh the available data, consider alternative possibilities, argue about relevance and worthiness, and then choose the best policy for the country or the best person for the office.

We do deliberate in that large sense sometimes, but what else do we do? What is going on in the parties and movements of the democratic political world besides deliberation?

The point of these questions is not to deny the importance of deliberation or to criticize theoretical accounts of what it requires, like that provided by Amy Gutmann and Dennis Thompson in *Democracy and Disagreement* or by Henry Richardson in *Democratic Autonomy*.[2] Nor do I mean to suggest that those three, or any other theorists of deliberation, would deny the importance of the activities that I shall list in my answer—although they might describe them somewhat differently. I mean to offer, in almost all the cases, a realistic (down-to-earth) and strongly sympathetic description.

My main purpose is to figure out how deliberation fits into a democratic political process that is, as my list makes clear, pervasively nondeliberative. So let's assume the value of "reasoning together" as Gutmann and Thompson describe it, where reason is qualified by reciprocity, publicity, and accountability. Politics has other values in addition to, often in tension with, reason: passion, commitment, solidarity, courage, and competitiveness (all of which also require qualification). These values are exemplified in a wide range of activities in the course of which men and women sometimes find occasion to reason together but which are better described in other terms.

I have fashioned my list to distinguish each item as sharply as possible from the idea of deliberation. But I don't mean to set up any sort of radical opposition, only to stress important differences, and I will come back to the ways we deliberate, or at least argue, in the course of all these other activities. I have to separate things out first, then deal with their various entanglements.

1. *Political education.* People have to learn how to be political. Some of what they learn is taught, or should be taught, in school: a rough history of democratic politics, including crucial events and actors; basic information about the federal system, the three branches of government, and the structure and timing of elections; perhaps an account of the leading ideologies, at least in caricature, and so on. But parties, movements, unions, interest groups, and ethnic and religious communities also educate their members, teaching them the ideas that the groups are organized to sustain or advance. What the old Communist parties called agitprop is a form of political education. Theorists committed to deliberation will say that this is a bad form of education, that it is really indoctrination; and parties, movements, and communities of many different sorts do seek to indoctrinate their members—to bring them to accept a doctrine—and, whenever possible, to represent it in public places, to repeat its central tenets (even when it is unpopular to do that), so

that each indoctrinated member becomes an agent of doctrinal transmission. Whether this sort of thing is good or bad, it is enormously important in political life because the political identity of most people or, better, of most of the people engaged by politics, is shaped in this way. This is how they become agents with opinions. Political identities are also shaped by familial life: agents with opinions marry agents with similar opinions and raise children to whom they try, most often successfully, to pass on those opinions. Socialization in the family, the earliest form of political education, is just agitprop with love. But the opinions that are transmitted reflect doctrines developed outside the family and inculcated in public settings through a great variety of public media.

2. *Organization.* One of the aims of political education, or, at least, of agitprop and indoctrination, is to induce people to identify with and work for particular organizations. Organizing itself is a more specific activity, which involves getting people actually to sign up, carry a card, accept a discipline, pay their dues, and learn to act in accordance with a script that they don't write themselves. (This sort of thing goes on throughout civil society, but I am focused here only on its political version.) The line that I have already quoted from one of the folksongs of the American left, "The union makes us strong!" is a democratic maxim; it reflects democracy's majoritarianism, which puts a premium on association and combination. Unions, like armies, are not strong if their members stop to deliberate about every action that the leadership commands. The leaders deliberate on behalf of everyone else, and this process is more or less public so that the members can speculate about what the deliberations of the leaders will come to—and they can sometimes object. But organizers try to persuade people to act in unison rather than as speculating or deliberating individuals.

3. *Mobilization.* Large-scale political action requires more than organization. Individual men and women have to be stimulated, provoked, energized, excited, called to arms. The military metaphor

is appropriate: an army can be an inert organization, held in reserve, the soldiers sitting in camps, cleaning their weapons, occasionally exercising. If they are to fight a war, they have to be mobilized. Something similar is true in political life. Ordinary members must be turned into militants, at least for the duration of a particular campaign. An especially intense sort of agitprop is necessary here, to capture their interest, focus their energies, draw them tightly together—so that they actually read the party's manifesto, argue on its behalf, and march, carry banners, and shout slogans in the party's parades. The image of masses of people shouting slogans will suggest to deliberative democrats an antidemocratic politics. But the character of the politics depends on the slogans, and these have often been pro-democratic. Indeed, what might be called the struggle for deliberative democracy—that is, for political equality, a free press, the right of association, civil rights for minorities, and so on—has required a lot of slogan shouting. It is not easy to imagine a democratic politics to which popular mobilization has become superfluous. (Whether that should be our ideal is a question I will come to at the end of my list.)

4. *Demonstration.* The point of a democratic mobilization is not to storm government offices and seize state power but to demonstrate personal intensity, numerical strength, and doctrinal conviction—all of which are critical to popular power. Hence the march or parade, the party rally, the placards and banners, the shouting of the participants, the oratory of the leaders, and the fierce applause it is meant to elicit. There is no room here for quiet deliberation, for that would not show the world the force of these people's concern, their passionate commitment and solidarity, their determination to achieve a particular political result. Their aim is to deliver a message—sometimes more generally to fellow citizens, sometimes more narrowly to an entrenched elite. The message goes like this: Here we stand; this is what we believe must be done; and we don't believe it casually, it isn't an opinion of the sort that might be cap-

tured by an opinion poll, it's not what we think today and might or might not think tomorrow; we will keep coming back until we have won; and if you want to get on with the ordinary business of politics, you had better accommodate us on this point (or on this series of seventeen points). Of course, all this can be said in a fanatical way, reflecting ideological or religious absolutism rather than political determination. But demonstrating intensity and conviction doesn't preclude negotiating later on, and the combination can be, and has been, used in defense of democratic rights—to vote, or strike, or associate freely—as well as in defense of substantive but contested reforms like prohibition, or gun control, or the minimum wage.

5. *Statement.* Making a statement is the aim of the demonstration, but statements can also take a more literal form. I have already mentioned the party manifesto, which militants endorse and repeat. Sometimes it is politically useful to reduce the manifesto to a credo or declaration—affirming this or that ideological conviction (something like the profession of faith of a religious community) or staking out a position on some more immediate issue—and then ask people to sign on. The publication of the credo, with names attached, signals to the world the commitment of these people, their readiness to take a stand in a public way. The authors of the credo may have deliberated about what to say, or, more likely, how to say it; the people asked to sign presumably deliberate about whether to sign. But the credo itself has the form of an assertion, which is not likely to be modified as a result of counterassertions. At moments of intense political conflict, newspapers and magazines will be filled with statements of this sort—declarations for and against this or that policy, say—but all of them taken together do not constitute democratic deliberation, because the different sets of authors and signatories don't always make arguments, and when they do, they rarely read each other's arguments (although they are certain to study the lists of names).

6. *Debate*. Statement and counterstatement make for a debate of sorts, although we usually expect debaters to speak directly to each other, arguing back and forth in a quicker, more spontaneous, more heated way than is possible in the exchange of credos and declarations. Debaters do have to listen to each other, but listening does not produce a deliberative process. Their object is not to reach an agreement among themselves but to win the debate, to persuade the audience that this position, rather than any of the alternatives, is the best one. (Some members of the audience may then deliberate among themselves or within themselves—going over the different positions in their own minds.) A debate is a contest between verbal athletes, and the aim is victory. The means are the exercise of rhetorical skill, the mustering of favorable evidence and the suppression of unfavorable evidence, the discrediting of the other debaters, the appeal to authority or celebrity, and so on. All these are plain to see in party debates in parliaments and assemblies and in debates between or among candidates at election time. But they are also standard on the lecture circuit and in newspapers and magazines whenever representatives of different positions are challenged to engage each others' arguments. The others are rivals, not fellow participants; they are already committed, not persuadable; the objects of the exercise, again, are the people in the audience—although many of them have come just to cheer for their own side, which can also be a useful political activity.

7. *Bargaining*. Sometimes the positions defended in this or that demonstration or manifesto or debate have been deliberated on, but more often they are the products of long and complicated negotiations among interested and opinionated individuals. That means that they don't represent anyone's idea of the best position; they are compromises with which no one is entirely satisfied; they reflect the balance of forces, not the weight of arguments. Commonly, bargaining doesn't begin until the relative strength of the different parties has been tested; sometimes its purpose is to avoid further costly or

bloody tests. So the parties agree to split the difference between them, the precise split depending on the previous tests of strength.[3] Balanced tickets are worked out the same way. Government policy in a democracy is more often the result of a negotiating process of this sort than of a deliberative process. The preferred policy is the one that accommodates the largest number of interests or, better, that accommodates precisely those interests that are able to assert themselves politically. (That's why organization and mobilization are so important, and why the state must sometimes help organize groups that have been discriminated against or repressed—the Wagner Act and the NLRB once again are useful examples.) I can imagine people arguing about how to serve the common good above and beyond all the particular interests, given the constraint that the particular interests must also be served. But that is a severe constraint, and the result is surely closer to give-and-take than to deliberation. Gutmann and Thompson argue that a deliberative democracy can tolerate bargaining when moral principle is not involved and when the parties "consider the merits of the collective results of their individual deals." But that can't be all they consider, or else they wouldn't be bargaining. And the outcome of their negotiation won't be determined by the collective value of this or that deal; it will be shaped by the particular interests involved (which the protagonists are sure to confuse with moral principles) and tested by political conflict.[4]

What distinguishes deliberation is better seen if we consider the example of the jury or the panel of judges. We don't want the jurors or judges in a criminal case bargaining with one another or even accommodating one another: "I'll vote your way on the first count if you vote my way on the second and third counts." We want them to weigh the evidence as best they can and come up with a verdict, that is, a true statement (*verum dictum*) about guilt or innocence. Politicians, in contrast, can legitimately act in exactly the way jurors and judges are barred from acting; indeed, a bargain is often the better part of political wisdom.

8. *Lobbying.* The cultivation of public officials by private parties is pervasive in politics, in both democratic and nondemocratic settings. In democracies the private parties are more likely to argue with the officials (rather than merely bargain with them) or, at least, to provide them with arguments, since democratically responsible officials have to defend their positions in one or another open forum. Still, lobbying at its most effective involves the forging of close personal relationships; it depends on individual friendships and social networks (which is why lobbying makes for inequality and has to be balanced by popular mobilization). Good lobbyists make up in charm, access, and insider knowledge whatever they lack in arguments. And the arguments they make often have less to do with the issue at hand than with the political future of the official they are lobbying.

9. *Campaigning.* Sometimes "campaigning," a military metaphor, is used to refer to any coordinated program of organizing, mobilizing, demonstrating, and so on, for a particular cause. Here I mean to describe only electoral campaigns, the democratic search for voter support. This involves most of the activities that I have listed so far, but it also has its own specific character—in part because it is focused on leaders with names, faces, and life histories as well as programs. It is these leaders who bear the brunt of the campaigning, soliciting the votes of their fellow citizens, making promises, trying to look trustworthy, and trying to suggest the untrustworthiness of their opponents. We can imagine them working within a set of limits—legal or moral rules defining, say, fair campaign practices—although virtually no effective limits exist today except those enforced by public opinion. What would the rules of a fair campaign be like? They would certainly bear little resemblance to the rules about what can and can't be said in a courtroom, and the reason for that, again, is that we don't believe that voters, any more than politicians, are like jurors or judges.

10. *Voting.* What should citizens do when they vote? Clearly, they should attend to the arguments being made by the different candidates and to the platforms of the parties. They should think about the consequences of this or that candidate's victory, not only for themselves but for the various groups to which they belong and for the country as a whole. Nonetheless, the body of citizens is not a search committee, deliberating on the most qualified candidate for the Senate, say, or the presidency. The members of a search committee are like jurors and judges in that they are assumed (sometimes wrongly) to have a common understanding of the relevant qualifications of the candidates and to deliberate impartially. Neither of those assumptions is justified in the case of citizens. Some of them may believe that toughness and commitment on this or that issue qualifies someone for the presidency, while others believe that the capacity to produce compromises on all issues is the best qualification. Some may identify with candidate X because he has defended their interests or their values in the past or with candidate Y because she is a member of their ethnic or religious community, or of their union or interest group, or because she has a political history similar to their own. Certainly, again, we want voters to consider the available evidence carefully and to reflect long and hard on the arguments of the contending candidates and parties. But they don't have to disqualify themselves if, because of their current interests or long-term commitments, they can't or won't pay equal attention to each of the contenders. Nor are they barred from choosing the issues on which they focus their attention for nondeliberative reasons. Indeed, voters have a right to choose issues and candidates alike with reference to their interests, passions, or ideological commitments, and most of them do just that. Perhaps it is a general truth that the issues on which citizens deliberate (or not) arise through a political process that is largely nondeliberative. It is through the mobilization of passions and interests that we are

forced to address what is (only now, because of the mobilization) the "question" of poverty, or corruption, or exploitation.

11. *Fund-raising.* Not much can be done in politics without money. Even before the age of television, money had to be raised to pay for salaries and offices; leaflets, newsletters, advertisements, and mass mailings; travel, meeting halls, and party conferences. Nothing is more common in political life than the varied activities that come under the rubric of fund-raising. Historically, in the United States these activities have probably provided the best examples of participatory democracy precisely because they don't involve studying the issues, arguing in public, making speeches, or sitting on deliberative committees. Of course, asking rich individuals for their money isn't the work of ordinary citizens, but fund-raising on a smaller scale—raffles, rummage sales, bake sales, dinners, passing the hat—is in fact a mass activity in which thousands of men and women are involved. And there can't be any doubt that money raised in this way is a bond: people who have given money and people who have helped to get it are more loyal to the cause, or loyal longer, than those who merely have reason to think that the cause is just.

12. *Corruption. Corruption* is a powerful censorious term describing a set of activities—outright bribery and extortion being the most obvious and probably the most common—that ought to be excluded from democratic politics. These activities, taken together, constitute my only negative example, and what I am interested in here is the argument for their exclusion. Bribery is certainly a nondeliberative activity (although its protagonists might well reason together about whom to bribe and how much to offer); more importantly, it is an activity that interferes with deliberation. That's why it is barred from some social and governmental settings, but not why it is barred from the primary political setting, the arena of electoral politics. Bribing judges and jurors is wrong precisely because it produces a result that doesn't reflect an impartial deliberative process.

Bribing government officials who dispense licenses and grants is wrong because it produces a result that doesn't reflect an honest search for qualified people and worthy projects. But bribing voters is wrong only because it interferes with the democratic representation of the voters themselves, not with any activity required of them: we don't get an accurate picture of their interests, concerns, or opinions. The result lacks democratic legitimacy, but not because impartial reason played no part in its production. A candidate who promises to reduce unemployment may be appealing to the unreflective interests of the unemployed, of working people who fear unemployment, and of all their friends and relatives, yet his appeal doesn't corrupt the political process. In fact, it is an important and entirely legitimate result of his appeal that we find out how many people share those particular interests and give them high priority. But he can't hire the unemployed to vote for him.

13. *Scut work*. A lot of what passes for political participation, a lot of the activity that is critical to the success of organizations and campaigns, is boring and repetitive work that has no intrinsically political character at all—like stuffing envelopes, setting up chairs, preparing placards, handing out leaflets, making phone calls (to ask for signatures or money, or to get people to go to meetings or to vote on election day), knocking on doors (for the same purposes), sitting at the literature table at party conferences. None of this requires much thought, although it often takes a lot of thought, and even some ingenuity, to organize the activity or to motivate oneself to do it. Since scut work is necessary—"someone has to do it"—it's worth dwelling for a moment on how it gets done. Commitment plays a major part, but I think it is important that this commitment is generated within a competitive system. The excitement of the competition, the sense of possible victory, the fear of defeat—all these press people to take on tasks they would otherwise be reluctant to perform. Even when politics begins to get dangerous, there isn't much difficulty in recruiting people to do scut work: danger

has its own excitements. Properly deliberative men and women, of course, might be reluctant to stuff envelopes even if no one was threatening to beat up all the envelope stuffers. They might be too busy reading position papers; they might be unmoved by competitive emotions. That scut work regularly gets done may well be the clearest example of the appeal of nondeliberative political activity.

14. *Ruling*. If scut work is the low end of politics, ruling is the high end. Aristotle defined citizenship in a democracy as "ruling and being ruled in turn." The first of these is commonly more valued; the acceptance of being ruled is an accommodation to democratic doctrine. If everyone is to have the experience of ruling, we have to take turns. In practice, of course, some people rule for long periods of time; others are ruled all the time. What distinguishes democratic ruling from undemocratic domination is the legitimation of the rulers through consent. But whether legitimate or not (and there is domination even in democracies), most rulers find ruling a pleasurable activity. Aristotle probably believed that part of the pleasure derived from the exercise of reason on a large scale, over the whole agenda of public issues. In this sense, ruling is a deliberative activity. But the pleasures of command are by no means wholly rational, or else people would not seek to rule with such passion. Sometimes, too, we want rulers who are not likely to deliberate too much—whose "native hue of resolution" is not, like Hamlet's, "sicklied o'er with the pale cast of thought."

That is my list, and it is a hard question whether, if I had not started by asking, What else? deliberation would have a place on it. Does deliberation belong in the same series that includes organization, mobilization, demonstration, and the rest? If we take what jurors or judges do as the model of a deliberative process, it probably doesn't.[5] True, courts are political institutions insofar as they exist within complex constitutional structures, and judges sometimes find themselves in conflict with officials exercising legislative and executive authority. But political considerations are supposed to be ruled out when a civil or criminal trial is in progress. The reason for ruling them out is the assumption we standardly make that there is a single just outcome of the trial, which jurors and judges are, or should be, united in pursuing. No such assumption is possible in political life, which is not merely adversarial but inherently and permanently conflictual. Very few political decisions are verdicts in the literal sense of that term. I don't mean that we can't sometimes insist that it is morally right and perhaps imperative to do X; but even the people who agree on the necessity of doing X are likely to disagree about how to do it, or how soon, or at whose expense.

It isn't necessary to adopt Carl Schmidt's view of politics as a form of war to recognize that different interests and ideological commitments are often irreconcilable. Parties in conflict do negotiate, settle, and then reconcile themselves to the settlement; but they are likely to feel that something has been lost in the negotiating process and to reserve the right to reopen the discussion whenever conditions seem propitious. We protect criminals against second prosecutions for the same crime, but we don't protect politicians against repeated challenges on the same issue. Permanent settlements are rare in political life precisely because we have no way of reaching a verdict on contested issues. Passions fade; men and women disengage from particular commitments; interest groups form new alignments; the world turns. But certain deep disagreements, like those between left and right, capital and labor, are remarkably persistent, and local forms of religious or ethnic conflict are often so embedded in a political culture as to seem natural to the participants. So politics is the endless return to these disagreements and conflicts, the struggle to manage and contain them and, at the same time, to win whatever temporary victories are available. The democratic way to win is to educate, organize, and mobilize more people than the other side does. "More" is what makes the victory legitimate, and while legitimacy is strengthened if good arguments can be made about the substantive issues at stake, the victory is rarely won by making good arguments.

Shouldn't we at least begin by making the best arguments that we can? Theorists of deliberation claim that this is something like a moral requirement; it is entailed by our recognition of others as rational men and women, capable of seeing the force of our claims or persuading us of the force of their claims, although this is always taken to be less likely. There is, however, another way of recognizing the others: not only as individuals who are rational in exactly the same way that we are but also as members of groups with beliefs and interests that mean as much to them as our beliefs and interests mean to us. If deliberation follows from the first of these recognitions, bargaining and compromise follow from the second. In political life, it is the second that is more often appropriate, even morally appropriate: the better we understand the differences that exist, and respect the people on the other side, the more we will see that what we need is not a rational agreement but a modus vivendi.

If the permanence of conflict helps account for the centrality of the activities on my list, so, more particularly, does the prevalence of inequality. Political history, when its telling isn't governed by ideology, is mostly the story of the slow creation or consolidation of hierarchies of wealth and power. People fight their way to the top of these hierarchies and then contrive to maintain their position. The ruling class may be much less coherent than Marxist theory suggests; nonetheless, something like it exists, with more or less self-awareness, and aims to sustain itself. Similarly, the associations of civil society are ruled by elites of various sorts, who also aim at permanence (even when particular officeholders are eager to escape the burdens they have voluntarily taken on). Popular organization, mass mobilization, and group solidarity are the only ways to oppose this aim. Their effect is not to level the hierarchies—at least it never has been—but only to shake them up, bring new people in, and perhaps set limits on the differentiations they define and entrench. So democratic politics makes possible an amended version of political history: now it is the story of the establishment *and partial disestablishment* of inequality. I don't see any way to avoid the endless repetition of this story, although no doubt some establishments are worse than others and some disestablishments are more fully realized. More specifically, I see no way to replace the endlessly renewed struggle for disestablishment with a deliberative process.

Deliberative democracy is definitely an egalitarian theory. It presupposes the equality of the men and women who speak and deliberate, and from this starting point, it generates and justifies egalitarian decisions. The process is consciously designed to avoid the charge that the best thinking of the best thinkers, deliberating under the best conditions, reflects nothing more than the interests of the powers that be ("the ideas of the ruling class are . . . the ruling ideas").[6] A proper deliberative process excludes those powerful interests altogether—by requiring the participants to imagine themselves deliberating behind a veil of ignorance, for example—or it balances interests by guaranteeing that all of them, including those of weak and oppressed groups, are equally represented in the discussions. But all this is accomplished in utopian time and space, while in the real world, the theory of deliberative democracy seems to devalue the only kind of politics that could ever establish a practical egalitarianism. As I have said, its protagonists start as equals, but they have never fought for that precarious status (and how they might attain it is not the subject of the theory). So their idealized discussions are not likely to be realized, or to be effective, in any actually existing political order.

Should we aim at realizing such idealized discussions? Is this our utopia, the dream of committed democrats—a world where political conflict, class struggle, and cultural difference are all replaced by pure deliberation? As Joseph Schwartz has recently argued in a book named for its thesis, *The Permanence of the Political*, liberal and left-wing theorists have often written as if this were their ultimate goal.[7] Thus the Marxist argument: conflict arises because of difference and hierarchy, and once the class struggle has been won and a classless society established, once difference has been transcended and hierarchy destroyed, the state will wither away and "the government of men" will be replaced by "the administration of things"; the age of politics will be over. Theories of this sort, Schwartz rightly claims, reflect a failure to understand (let alone to relish) the many and varied forms of cultural diversity and social conflict. It is the uneasiness with difference, above all, that prompts the dislike of politics and the fantasy of abolishing it. The abolition is unlikely to be achieved, however, except by repressing both difference and conflict, which would require a highly coercive politics. I am sure that repression would be undertaken only in defense of ideas that the theorists and their friends had thought about long and hard, in imperfect but not implausible deliberative settings like academic seminars or communities of exiled intellectuals or the committees of vanguard parties far from political power. Still, committed democrats can hardly endorse the repression—or the inequality it so obviously involves.

Deliberation does have a place, an important place, in democratic politics, but I don't think that it has an independent place— a place of its own. There is no setting in the political world quite like the jury room, in which we don't want people to do anything *except* deliberate. Similarly, although politics is often said to involve committee work more than anything else, there are no political committees quite like a search committee looking to appoint a professor or a prize committee trying to identify the best novel of the year. The work of searching out candidates and awarding prizes is often politicized, but when it is, the results are likely to be called into question. By contrast, we expect political considerations to prevail in the committees of a party or movement and even in legislative and administrative committees. At least, such considerations are legitimately invoked; something would be wrong with the democratic process if they had no role at all. Imagine a group of bureaucrats deliberating with great seriousness for many hours and then doing what they have concluded is the right thing to do—without taking into account the recorded preferences of a majority of the people or the interests of whatever coalition of groups currently constitutes the majority. Imagine that they ignore all personal preferences and interests, just as juries are supposed to do. The chosen policy of the deliberating bureaucrats might well be the best one, but it would not be the right policy for a democratic government.

Democracy requires deliberation, which is to say, a culture of argument, and it requires a body of citizens who are open, at least in principle (and some of the time in practice), to the best arguments. But arguing can't be isolated from all the other things that citizens do. There is no such thing as pure argument, deliberation in itself, and no set of people whose work it is or ever could be. In most of the disputes that go on in political life, neither is there a single best argument that is or ought to be equally persuasive to people with different worldviews, religious beliefs, economic interests, and social standing. Hence there is no outcome that is purely deliberative, as opposed to political in the full sense of that term.

Deliberation's proper place is dependent on activities that it doesn't constitute or control. We make room for it, and should do that, in the larger space that we provide for more properly political activities. We try to introduce a certain measure of calm reflection and reasoned argument into, say, the work of political education. Even agitprop can be better or worse, and it is clearly better if its arguments are honestly informed and addressed to the most difficult challenges that the party or movement confronts. Similarly, we can imagine the party platform drawn up by a group of people who are not only good negotiators but reflective men and women, who aim at proposals that are morally justified and economically realistic as well as politically appealing. We can imagine a negotiating process in which people try to understand and accommodate the interests of the other side (while still defending their own) rather than just driving the hardest possible bargain. We can imagine parliamentary debates where the rival speakers listen to one another and are prepared to modify their positions. And finally, we can imagine citizens who actually think about the common good when they evaluate candidates, or party programs, or the deals their representatives strike, or the arguments they make.

None of these imaginings is far-fetched, even if they are only rarely realized. Indeed, at a somewhat lower level, the existing democracy is already a culture of argument; loyal scut workers, for example, talk about politics while they sit stuffing envelopes, and disagree fiercely about whether another mass mailing is what the movement most needs at this moment. Nothing that I have said is meant to denigrate discussions of this sort—or of a "higher" sort. Yes, those of us who want to defend the idea of a more egalitarian society must argue that such a society is possible and sketch a picture of what it might look like, which should be as plausible (and as inspiring) as we can make it. This is our utopia. But the arguments and sketches will be utopian in the bad sense—sentimental and self-indulgent descriptions of nowhere—unless we also mobilize the men and women who experience, or at least sympathize with, the injuries of class and the traumas of stigma and subordination. These people, too, should join in the arguments about the common good, and about equality, and about strategies for increasing equality—but only alongside and together with their engagement in the more material work of politics.

My hope for deliberation alongside and together with other things is more likely to be realized if political activity is carried out in the open, with full publicity, by activists and officials who are democratically accountable. If democracy requires argument, the culture of argument is enhanced and strengthened by the standard democratic institutions and practices—elections, party competition, a free press. Are there other practical arrangements that might help citizens, or force them, to think about the common good? This is an important question, addressed inventively by James Fishkin in a number of recent books.[8] But I don't believe that these arrangements, whatever they are, can or should substitute for the activities on my list. Fishkin argues for the establishment of citizens' juries, which would be asked to decide, or at least to propose solutions for, critical issues of public policy. In forming the juries, scientific sampling would replace the usual forms of electoral politics, and in the jury meetings, rational discussion would replace the usual forms of political debate. To me, this example suggests the central problem of deliberative democracy: deliberation in itself is not an activity for the demos.[9] I don't mean that ordinary men and women don't have the capacity to reason, only that 300 million of them, or even one million or a hundred thousand, can't plausibly reason together. And it would be a great mistake to turn them away from the things that they can do together. For there would then be no effective, organized opposition to the established hierarchies of wealth and power. The political outcome of such a turning is readily predictable: the citizens who turned away would lose the fights they probably want, and might well need, to win.

In the next, and last, chapter, I will expand on an argument only suggested in this one: that the passionate engagement of large numbers of people is necessary to a democratic and egalitarian politics. Political passion is something that liberal theorists have always worried about and mostly frowned upon, not without reason. Yet a passionless politics has dangers of its own—not least among them, the danger of defeat.

SIX

Politics and Passion

THERE IS A HIDDEN ISSUE AT THE HEART OF contemporary debates about nationalism, identity politics, and religious fundamentalism. The issue is passion. Opponents of these phenomena fear the vehement rhetoric, the unthinking engagement, the rage against opponents that they associate with the appearance of passionate men and women in the political arena. They associate passion with collective identification and religious belief—both of which lead people to act in ways that can't be predicted by any rational account of their interests and that don't follow from any rationally defensible set of principles.

Interests can be negotiated, principles can be debated, and negotiations and debates are political processes that, in practice as well as in theory, set limits on the behavior of those who join them. But passion, on this view, knows no limits, sweeps all before it. Faced with contradiction or conflict, it presses inexorably toward violent resolutions. Politics properly understood, politics in its reasonable and liberal version, is a matter of calm deliberation — or, if the argument of the last chapter is at least partially accepted, of organized competition, calculated trade-offs, and hard bargains. Passion, by contrast, is impetuous, unmediated, all-or-nothing.

Yet, in so many parts of the world, including our own parts, large numbers of people are both politically engaged and passionate in their engagement. The spectacle is often frightening. I don't want to deny the fear (or to deny being afraid). It's not just the all-too-frequent newspaper stories about negotiations broken off, debates interrupted, angry leaders storming out of committee meetings. It's not just that so many people are marching under the banners of identity and faith (rather than economic interest or political principle). Passion is also mobilized for internecine ethnic and religious conflict, where it leads to terrible cruelty: terrorist attacks, "ethnic cleansing," rape, and massacre. Passion makes for war, not of all against all, every person against every other (for the war that Thomas Hobbes describes is a rational activity, produced by universal distrust), but of some against some, group against group, where sheer hatred is the animating force.

How should we understand all this? I shall begin by asking how we do understand it. What is our mind's picture of the place of passion in political life? The most popular picture among contemporary liberal intellectuals and academics, political and social theorists, journalists and commentators (looking at Bosnia or Rwanda, say), is nicely suggested by these famous lines from William Butler Yeats's poem "The Second Coming."

> Things fall apart; the centre cannot hold;
> Mere anarchy is loosed upon the world,
> The blood-dimmed tide is loosed, and everywhere
> The ceremony of innocence is drowned;
> The best lack all conviction, while the worst
> Are full of passionate intensity.[1]

I first heard these lines quoted long ago, in the early 1950s, during the McCarthy years, and I imagined, until I was told otherwise, that Yeats was a contemporary American poet: he seemed to be writing about my own time, which I assumed was also his. I suspect that the poem often has that kind of resonance (it was translated into German, in Princeton, New Jersey, by Erich Kahler, a refugee from Nazism, for whom I am certain it had that kind of resonance), and so I am going to use it as my text.[2] I shall try to understand passion in politics, or begin to understand it, by considering the meaning and impact of Yeats's lines. But I will also keep in mind the actual appearance in the world of the people Yeats calls "best" and "worst."

He suggests an explanation of those appearances, or, perhaps more precisely, those of us who think we belong with the best infer an explanation, characteristically self-critical. We are the reason the center cannot hold; the fault lies in our own moral and intellectual weakness. We have lost conviction about our interests and principles, so we cannot confront and overcome the passionate intensity of the others. The distinction between us and them is clear. We are educated, intelligent, liberal, and reasonable people, and when our convictions are strong, so is society as a whole. When the world makes sense, when order is understood and justice defended, when the common decencies prevail, we constitute the center and hold all unruliness in check. Passion is associated with the others, the blood-dimmed tide surging in when the center collapses. At any given moment, it is easy to identify the tide—or at least to point at it; social analysis is always more controversial—and the poem seems to be suggesting that we should, but probably can't, summon up the conviction necessary to turn it back.

Yeats himself probably did not intend his lines to be read as I have just read them. According to Yvor Winters's persuasive interpretation of the poem, which places it in the context of both Irish politics and Yeats's personal world-historical mythology, the people

Yeats had in mind as worst were the Dublin politicians trying, in the aftermath of the Easter Uprising of 1916, to establish a democratic state in Ireland and to set themselves at its head (the poem was written in 1919 or 1920). And the word *best* refers, as is only linguistically proper, to the old Anglo-Irish aristocracy, whose members lacked the will to take control in those difficult years.[3] But the point of the poem is not to criticize their weakness; the triumph of the worst is necessary to open the way for transformation—one of those great cyclical transformations that Yeats believed gave shape to human history. The "beast slouching toward Bethlehem" in the poem's last lines, which explain its title, signals a new age and a new barbarism, out of which a new aristocracy will be born. Passionate intensity drives the process, not so much forward (Yeats was certainly not a Whig or a progressive mythologist) as onward to destruction and rebirth.

That description of the poet's intention may be right or wrong, but readers have never been bound by authorial intention, and I will not be bound by it here. That's not what the poem means for us. Characteristically, we give the poem a moralizing and politicizing meaning, which serves, above all, to condemn passionate intensity and then to decry, or perhaps only to mourn, the failure of conviction. This is the meaning, the use, of the poem that I want to examine and criticize.

Note first that the terms are not reversible: the poem, on this reading, doesn't suggest that it would be a good thing if the worst lacked all conviction and the best were full of passionate intensity. The poem's associations of goodness and conviction, on the one hand, and of badness and passion, on the other, follow from the standard polarized meaning of those terms. I don't want to say that being best and having convictions go together. Being best and not having convictions also go together. Skepticism, irony, doubt, a critical cast of mind—all these are also the marks of the best people (although, again, Yeats probably thought of them as signs of aristocratic decadence). It is admirable to have convictions, but it is also admirable not to be too certain about them. The best people are not true believers, or members of the party of orthodoxy, or ideologically correct sectarians, for that way lies passionate intensity. A certain political weakness is built into conviction, for, on this reading of the poem, it rests on reason and so is always open to criticism and disproof. Moral conviction may be native to aristocrats, but it is also a sign of their noble quality when they worry endlessly about whether they should act on their convictions, when their resolution is "sicklied o'er with the pale cast of thought." And then we worry in turn about their capacity for leadership.

The worst people, by contrast, especially when they are intellectuals, as they often are, don't have convictions at all but beliefs, doctrines, dogmas, and ideologies. All these lend themselves to certainty, and certainty, when it is militant, is also passionate and intense. I suppose that the passionate intensity of the worst is more often expressed in nonintellectual or anti-intellectual terms, as bigotry and prejudice. But these are both the offspring of doctrine. The members of one group will not hate the members of another in the relevant way, the way that collapses the center and sets loose the blood-dimmed tide, unless the second group has been condemned in doctrinal terms, through some genetic or genealogical account of its inferiority, say, or some historical account of its crimes. To associate passionate intensity with ignorance is a common mistake. In fact, the worst are always at least half-educated; they make up what we might think of as the petty bourgeoisie of intellectual life. They have learned belief but not skepticism. Alternatively, they lack the natural modesty of the best, whose innermost thought is that they might be wrong, and who have acquired, by long reflection on that possibility, the virtues of ambivalence and tolerance.

So it isn't the case that the worst lack reason, but rather that their reason is distorted by faith and dogma, whereas the reason of the best is tempered by doubt or, perhaps, by humility. The politi-

cal result is what Yeats describes. The worst possess the courage of
their certainty; the best, at best, the courage of their uncertainty.
The political contest between them is bound to be unequal.

It wasn't always unequal. The poem describes the present moment, our own here and now, and what it suggests is that we live in
the latter days of some historical process (not necessarily a Yeatsian
cycle). The cry that the center doesn't hold is a lament about late-
ness in time. Once the center did hold—else we wouldn't know that
it is the center. I am not sure how to describe that earlier age, but the
standard accounts of it are not entirely fantastic. The worst were
indeed ignorant then, and passively subordinate because of their
ignorance—and therefore better than they are today: they knew
their place. The convictions of the best were as yet untempered by
doubt, not so much because of their belief in God or nature or history as because of their belief in themselves. (So perhaps there is
some truth in the Yeatsian mythology, which associates the stable
center with a young but established aristocracy.) The worst were
humble in those days, and the best were self-confident.

That is the picture that Yeats's poem evokes or can be used to
evoke. It must seem strange to connect it in any way with liberal political theory, especially since Yeats himself stood so far to the right;
but that is what I mean to do. (I will turn to a more standard liberal
view later on.) Although liberalism looks forward to a time when all
men and women participate in a democratic process of rational decisionmaking, its uneasiness with and disparagement of passion ties
it back into an older political-philosophical tradition in which the
enlightened few anxiously watch the teeming, irrational masses and
dream of a former time when its members were passive, deferential,
politically apathetic. Yeats's phrase "passionate intensity" recalls,
for example, David Hume's critique of "enthusiasm," which Hume
identified in his *History of England* with the Protestant sects of the
seventeenth century.[4] Hume believed that reason was the slave of

the passions, but religious zeal was one passion that he hoped reasonable men and women would resist. In this tradition (Hume is useful because he suggests its Whiggish version), any strong emotional commitment is taken to be dangerous, a threat to the social stability and political order that allows for mental cultivation, artistic achievement, and what we might call moral grace—the virtues of a gentleman and a scholar. No doubt, these virtues have their own history, which I shall not pursue here. I want to focus instead on the argument in which they play a part, an argument that responds, I believe, to the appearance of populist religion and political radicalism.

Yeats's powerful line "Things fall apart; the centre cannot hold" plays off of John Donne's earlier lines:

> 'Tis all in peeces, all cohaerence gone;
> All just supply, and all Relation;
> Prince, Subject, Father, Sonne, are things forgot.[5]

This is what follows when "New philosophy calls all in doubt." The argument is more intellectual than in Yeats, although the forgetting of the social hierarchy is an allusion not to the scientific revolution but to Protestant radicalism—the two probably connected for Donne, who says later in his "First Anniversary" that "a Hectique feaver hath got hold / Of the whole substance [of the world]." Donne did not live to see the blood-dimmed tide awash in the streets of London, but that is the specific experience of things falling apart, the world in pieces, that these poems evoke or, again, can be used to evoke. Hectique feaver, enthusiasm, and passionate intensity are the marks of the plebeian others (and also of their "organic intellectuals")—in these poems, the commonly understood reference is to the lower orders, but it can readily shift to pariah peoples, enslaved races, and conquered nations. It is when such groups rebel (whether their demand is for emancipation, recognition, or empowerment) that the blood-dimmed tide is loosed and

the "ceremonies of innocence"—all the common courtesies, celebrations, and rituals through which social coherence is enacted—
are drowned in the flood.

This argument has an obvious appeal because it offers an obvious truth. Who can doubt that Puritan repression, French revolutionary terror, Stalinist purges, and contemporary nationalist massacres and deportations were and are the work of passionately
intense men and women—and their passions the worst ones: dog-
matic certainty, anger, envy, resentment, bigotry, and hatred? And
who can doubt that the failure of the moderates in each case, the
defenders of parliamentary democracy, civil liberty, and political
pluralism, has something to do with their liberal conviction and
lack of conviction (which come to the same thing) and their self-
doubt? Doesn't it follow that we must look for a way to eliminate
political passion and to make the better qualities of mind and
spirit—reasonableness, skepticism, irony, and tolerance—somehow triumphant in the political arena?

To replace heat with light: that would be a good thing to do if it
were possible to do it. But it isn't possible. To understand why, we
have only to think about politics as it really is. Terrorists and murderers, whatever their passionate intensity, are also driven by conviction, that is, by strong ideas about the world. No doubt, these derive from religious or political belief rather than from philosophical
reflection; no doubt, the intellectual standards of terrorists and
murderers are usually low. Still, they take their lead from the aristocrats of intellectual life. Calvin, Rousseau, Marx, and Nietzsche
have all been quoted at length by people they would be loath to acknowledge as disciples.

At the same time, the passionate intensity of terrorists and
murderers is at least sometimes matched by the passionate intensity of their most heroic and effective opponents. If there were
nothing awful to oppose, there would be no need for that kind of
emotional engagement. But opposition and conflict, disagreement

and struggle where the stakes are high—that's what politics is. I
don't want to say that that's what politics essentially is. I have never
been drawn to essentialist definitions of anything. Still, a noncon-
flictual politics is very hard to imagine, even when we see centrist
politicians pretending to have no disagreements with anyone. It is
possible, of course, to lower the stakes—which is often a good thing
to do—but not to zero. In Engels's "administration of things," the
things will have no stake at all in how they are administered, but this
is another antipolitical fantasy.[6] Surely administrators do well when
they follow their rational convictions, and their performance would
be further improved by a little irony and self-doubt. But political activists must be more passionately engaged, or else they will lose
every struggle for political power.

This is a general truth about politics, but it has special force in
an age when the old social hierarchies are challenged, when coherence is undermined, when the world is in pieces. For it is the passionate intensity of the many that poses the challenge, and once it
has been posed, ceremonies of innocence, all Relation, and sweet
reasonableness have only limited value. They won't make for a new
order; they won't lead men and women to accept the discipline required for innovation and reconstruction. "Nothing great was ever
achieved," wrote Ralph Waldo Emerson, "without enthusiasm."[7]
That statement is empirically verifiable, and the evidence for it is
overwhelming. Unhappily, it is equally true—the evidence is equally
overwhelming—that nothing terrible was ever achieved without
enthusiasm.

That double truth expresses the inherent risks of politics as a
purposive activity. Indeed, the risks reflect another doubling: not
just passion but reason, too, plays a part in both great and terrible
achievements. Every political and social advance requires rational
persuasion (whatever else it requires). But the vaulting ambition to
build a rational order, at any cost to the ignorant, unreasoning multitude, has produced its own forms of terrorism and murder. Just as

passionate activists quote philosophy, so philosophers are driven by passion. Members of both these groups serve sometimes in the army of the good and sometimes on the other side.

The risks of politics can be recklessly increased or cautiously reduced; but they cannot be avoided altogether, unless one gives up the hope for great achievements. And that is exactly what happens, I think, when conviction and passion, reason and enthusiasm, are radically split and when this dichotomy is locked onto the dichotomy of the holding center and the chaos of dissolution. The result is an ideology of risk-avoidance, which is also, willy-nilly, a defense of the status quo against all political demands from below. It is a peculiar ideology and an unlikely defense, because it can't, almost by definition, provide much inspiration; it can't move men and women to action—for that would require a passionate attachment to the way things are rather than a merely sad reflection on the way they were. The reflection is more an excuse for failure than a program for success, which explains why the poems I have quoted are written (or read) in the tones of lamentation. The status quo is defended only in retrospect, after all coherence is gone and things have fallen apart—as if to say, See how awful are the effects of passionate intensity. Wouldn't it have been better never to have loosed the blood-dimmed tide!

"The blood-dimmed tide": I have repeated this phrase because it is the key, not to the poem—I don't claim to have that key—but to the worldview the poem represents. How Yeats imagined the tide I can't say, but I know how we imagine it. The tide is the mob, and the blood of its members isn't dimmed but doing the dimming. Their blood is up, not down; they are excited, passionate, looking to shed the blood of their enemies. We imagine a mob drunk with enthusiasm: enraged, resentful, and envious plebeians; or religious fanatics; or blood and soil nationalists. And the worst among them are the demagogues at their head, who are seen here not as cynical manipulators, Machiavellian princes, but as men and women who fully share the passions of the people they lead. That's what passionate intensity means: the emotions are genuine, which is why they are so frightening.

But this is the hostile version of the story; it is true but one-sided, focused emphatically on the risks of passion (and not at all on the risks of reason). Think now about some of the people who have challenged established social orders: nineteenth-century workers demonstrating for the right to organize; feminist agitators chaining themselves to lampposts and assaulting the police in England in the first decades of the twentieth century; civil rights marchers, black and white, in the American South in the 1960s; their counterparts in Northern Ireland in the 1970s; "velvet" revolutionaries in the streets of Prague in 1989. This list is meant to be persuasive. Yet there must have been people who thought that what they were watching—workers, agitators, marchers—was the blood-dimmed tide. I am inclined to say flatly that they were wrong and that the passion-conviction dichotomy can make no sense of these cases. What we see in all of them is conviction energized by passion and passion restrained by conviction. And isn't this the more likely story—I don't mean in its attractiveness but in its denial of the dichotomy? The same story can be told just as well about leaders and followers far less appealing than the men and women of the labor, feminist, and civil rights movements or of the 1989 revolutions. Indeed, that is the real story. Ironic, indecisive, Hamlet-like moderates and impassioned, bloodthirsty mobs do appear in the historical record, but organized parties and movements of many different sorts, good and bad, are far more common. Politics has mostly to do with people who have both conviction and passion, reason and enthusiasm, in always unstable combination. The distinctions we make among them, the lines we draw, the sides we choose, are not determined by the Yeatsian dichotomies but by the different ends these people pursue, the different means they adopt in the pursuit, and the different ways they relate to one another. Once we have made our choices, why shouldn't we hope for a world in which the people we oppose are haunted by their lost convictions while we are full of passionate intensity?

I want now to tell a different story about passion in politics, one that has more obvious liberal connections and that addresses, as I have not yet done, the moral and psychological accommodation that liberal theorists have made with at least some passions. This second story is suggested by Albert Hirschman's *The Passions and the Interests* and Joseph Schumpeter's theory of imperialism, which Hirschman invokes at the end of his book.[8] Although its terms are still radically dichotomous, they are also recast to reflect a sociology (and perhaps also a class interest) rather different from that reflected in the argument I have used Yeats's poem to exemplify.

The Yeatsian argument describes the social world with a set of oppositions:

conviction	passion
aristocrats	plebeians
enlightened few	blood-dimmed tide

The alternative argument begins by associating passion with war and warlike activity and then with the aristocracy, whose historical legitimacy, after all, is based on success in battle. The ideal aristocrat is committed to the display of courage and the pursuit of honor and glory, and these are best realized in the course of military triumph. Ideally, again, aristocrats fight only against dragons; they rescue innocents in peril; they defend their country. In practice, however, their heroic exuberance overflows into wars of aggression and conquest (hence Schumpeter's claim that aristocratic values are one of the sources of imperialist politics). Like Plato's guardians, aristocrats must be men of spirit, which is to say that they must be passionate, and in battle, passionately intense. This intensity isn't confined to foreign wars; although Plato hoped that his guardians would be fierce abroad and gentle at home, aristocratic passion also makes for civil war, and even in times of peace, aristocrats are likely to run riot, fight duels, lord it over their social inferiors.[9] Hirschman finds this view of the aristocracy mostly in eighteenth-century texts, but it already appears in the cities of Renaissance Italy. "If we consider the objects of the nobles and of the people," writes Machiavelli in his *Discourses,* "we must see that the first have a great desire to dominate, whilst the latter have only the wish not to be dominated . . . to live in the enjoyment of liberty."[10]

Aristocrats are dangerous men. Perhaps I should say, aristocratic men are dangerous. Despite the common identification of passion with womankind in both religious and secular discourse, women are so radically excluded from the political sphere that the embodiments of passionate intensity in both political action and argument are regularly male. A certain pre-political sentimentality is often attributed to women, by men, and also an antipolitical, disruptive sexuality, but not a specifically political intensity. By contrast, the aristocrat's passion for glory, at least from the perspective of his merchant and artisan enemies, is described as a (male) lust for domination and blood.

The opposing figure is the good burgher calmly pursuing his profits, calculating advantage in the marketplace, getting and spending, enjoying his liberty. The burgher knows that both his trade and his enjoyment require peace; his instrumental rationality produces urban civility and what eighteenth-century writers called *doux commerce.* Of course, he, too, is driven by passion, but the passion for gain (and for enjoyment) leads people to act mostly within the constraints of law and order. In the literature that Hirschman examines, this passion is singled out and re-conceived as "interest," whereas the passion for glory retains its old name and its old connotations of unrestrainable enthusiasm, intensity, and violence. Samuel Johnson's claim that "there are few ways in which a man can be more innocently employed than in getting money" may, as Hirschman says, underestimate the social consequences of capitalism,[11] but it perfectly captures the spirit of my second story and sets up its alternative dichotomies:

war	commerce
passion	interest
aristocracy	bourgeoisie

What is most important here is the displacement of conviction (or principle or moral reason) by interest. There is something high-minded about conviction, which limits its social range. The standard association is with the best people, the enlightened few, whether these are conceived as the members of an aristocratic or an intellectual elite. But interests are more widely, indeed universally, possessed. We all have interests, and we are all employed in getting money (or in thinking about getting money), so we are all subject to the instrumental rationality of *doux commerce*. If a politics ruled entirely by conviction is difficult to imagine, a politics ruled by interest is easy to imagine.[12] This is the form that liberalism actually takes in the world; it is by recognizing interest that liberalism accommodates itself to the passions—while still excluding the fiercer forms of attachment and struggle. The politics of interested individuals and competing interest groups allows for conflict but stops well short of civil war; it explicitly sets the warlike passions, and implicitly the passions of affiliation, beyond the pale. Liberal writers rationalize this politics by calling it rational, which, indeed, it often is—and always should be. Tocqueville's defense of "self-interest properly understood" simply reinstates the reason-passion dichotomy, with all the old valences.[13]

The positive view of interest has been a standard feature of liberal thought since the eighteenth century—though some recent defenders of ideal speech and deliberative democracy seem to favor conviction. I think they think that interest is still too close to passionate intensity. By contrast, the identification of the aristocracy with passion, especially with violent passion, has had a much shorter history. It served a certain purpose in the class wars of the early modern period, but the victory of bourgeois liberalism, wherever it occurred, quickly produced a kind of aristocratic adaptation. Aristocrats became diplomats instead of warriors, taking over the foreign service of many of the new constitutional or republican regimes. In domestic society, they ruled the social register as patrons of high culture and arbiters of good taste. Alternatively, they figured in popular literature, and sometimes in the real world, as decadent, parasitic, and cynical "playboys" ("playgirls" come from a lower social class), driven by lust but definitely averse to blood. And then the dangerous passions have to be assigned a different social location.

The old plebeian location, however, is now contested territory, for it is one of the major achievements of Marxism to have established this simple truth—that the working class has rational interests—and so to require that passionate intensity be located somewhere else.[14] Although Marx obviously hoped that the workers would prove dangerous to their capitalist oppressors, they were not socially dangerous. In principle, and in fact, they would not set anarchy loose upon the world; they would produce their own forms of social coherence, their own ways of holding things together. Class consciousness was and is a rational discipline; Marxists, and leftists and liberals generally, argued that it would be proof against the forms of unreasoning passion that they identified with religion and nationalism. In the Marxist story, though not always in fact, religion and nationalism would find their most fervent supporters not in the working class but in the petty bourgeoisie and the lumpen proletariat.

This argument has been revived in recent years by critics of identity and empowerment politics. Class, they argue, makes for rational political behavior because it associates people on the basis of their common economic interests, in pursuit of an individualist emancipation, whereas ethnicity rests most deeply on birth and blood and then on the collective and irrational passions that these two generate—hence the relative restraint of the class struggle compared to ethnic warfare. The interests at stake in the first of these can always be compromised; the second is, like passion itself, all or nothing.[15] There is probably some truth in the comparisons this distinction makes possible, but not much. Anyone who lived for a while in the twentieth century saw class warfare, driven by envy, resentment, and paranoia, turned into a justification for purges and massacres, judicial torture and arbitrary imprisonment, concentration camps and forced labor. At the same time, movements for national liberation and racial and gender justice made rational appeals to the larger world and imposed moral constraints on their own activists.[16] So the argument falls apart. We have to work out better distinctions between the forms of class politics and racial/ethnic/gender politics that we like and those that we fear. The dichotomy of interest and passion is probably of even less use in doing that than the dichotomy of good and bad is. Our sense of goodness and badness is what really determines our judgments.

But if we identify good and bad passions by looking at the causes in which they are enlisted, and if we judge the causes rationally, haven't we, once again, reinstated the old dichotomy, with reason still supreme? Perhaps all that I have accomplished here is to admit more of our passionate life into the legitimate world. As the passion for gain was moved upward, as it were, into the realm of respectability, so now I have moved the passions of affiliation and combat into the same realm: the first of these, greed, as it used to be called, makes market behavior comprehensible; the second two, solidarity and hostility, explain a great deal of political behavior.[17] But all of them must still be rationalized—that is, as Tocqueville said, they must be properly understood and well directed—and they themselves, by themselves, provide no help with either the understanding or the direction.

So this is my argument so far: Passionate intensity has its legitimate place in the social world, not only when we are getting money but also when we are choosing allies and engaging opponents. This extension of rational legitimacy to the political passions seems to me a useful revision of liberal theory, which has been too preoccupied in recent years with the construction of dispassionate deliberative procedures. It opens the way for better accounts of social connection and conflict and for more explicit and self-conscious answers to the unavoidable political question: Which side are you on?

I think that the old dichotomy invites an even more radical denial. It's not that reason and passion can't be conceptually distinguished; I have been making that distinction throughout this chapter. They are, however, always entangled in practice—and this entanglement itself requires a conceptual account. So it is my ambition to blur the line between reason and passion: to rationalize (some of) the passions and to impassion reason. Our feelings are implicated, it seems to me, in the practical understanding as well as in the political defense of the good and even of the right. I am going to argue for this simple proposition without elaborating anything like a theoretical psychology. The point can be made with an illustration that appeals only to a commonsensical view of our feelings.

Consider the case of military aggression, which is often identified—by Schumpeter, for example—with the bad passions (a useful example of commonsense psychology). But our hostility to aggression is just as passionate as aggression itself. Behind that hostility, I believe, is a mental picture of people like ourselves living quietly and peacefully in their own places, in their homes and homeland. They are attacked without legitimate cause (that's the definition of aggression), their families and friends, their cities and towns, their way of life, threatened with destruction, perhaps destroyed. Surely our rational condemnation of the attack cannot be understood without reference to that mental picture. In fact, it derives from the picture; it depends on our emotional identification with those people, who are the projected images of the men and women with whom we ourselves live, at home and in peace. Identifications of this sort are the work of the affiliative passions, and they shape our response to aggression as surely as the passion for triumph and domination shapes the aggression itself. Passionate intensity is evident in the aims and the actions of both sides. And so is rational conviction, for the aggressors probably believe—at least they are likely to be told by their political friends and then to tell themselves—that they have a legitimate claim to the land they are attacking. "May I with right and conscience make this claim?" Shakespeare's Henry V asks the Archbishop of Canterbury before his invasion of France, and he is told, of course, that he may. The rest of us, rational observers all, are firmly convinced that violent border crossings like Henry's pose a universal threat. This is how things actually are: there are "good" and "bad" combinations of reason and passion, which we distinguish rationally and passionately.

Seen from a sufficient distance, the aggressors probably look like the blood-dimmed tide. Maybe they are a marauding band of irregular troops bent on rape and plunder. But they can as easily be, they more often are, a disciplined army whose military or political leaders are passionately focused on the act of conquest (they may also be rationally focused). Passionate intensity has, in fact, no fixed social form. It can be embodied equally well in marauders and in armies, in mobs and in movements. It also has no fixed social base. A particular set of passions (or reasons), in a particular time and place, may be connected with an economic class or ethnic group. But all such connections are unstable, and many of them are largely imaginary. The historical arguments that link passionate intensity with the plebeians or the aristocracy, or rational interest with the bourgeoisie or the working class, are themselves passionate and interested—ideological in the original sense of that word. Just as there is no psychological map, so there is no sociological map, that provides sure guidance for our political choices.

We still have to choose between the good and the bad. So what is it in the political world that these moral terms refer to? I have already answered that question as best I can, but let me now attempt a summary statement. What political scientists call decisionmaking is not the most important concern of politics. Political leaders do have to make decisions, of course, and I suppose that they should do so rationally and dispassionately. Even that is not entirely clear; many crimes have been committed by leaders who repress their sympathetic emotions and act in the name of a purely rational realpolitik. In any case, before these leaders can decide on important matters, they have to come to power; they have to organize a following, constitute a party, work out a program, campaign for wider support against other parties and programs, and win state office. This competition for power is the primary form of political life, which is best understood as the contest between organized and more or less strongly differentiated groups. I have described the democratic form of this contest (which Yeats seems to have disliked); it can take different forms. The basic idea is that without groups in conflict, there would be no politics at all, or nothing that we would recognize as politics.

So the crucial judgment that we have to make is not about what decision to favor but about what group to join (or to stick with or to leave). The crucial judgment is what the Italian writer Ignazio Silone called "the choice of comrades."[18] We make that choice, it seems to me, with reference to a complex and intricately interconnected set of criteria. The word *comrade* is helpful, even if it is currently out of fashion, because by suggesting that the group has strong affective ties it requires us to include the quality of those ties among the relevant criteria. Joining (or sticking with) a group of

comrades is not like getting in line at a ticket kiosk; it is not like joining Sartre's "series." It's not even like signing a statement in support of a candidate or policy, where we add our names to a list of
names mostly unknown to us. Choosing comrades involves emotional as well as moral or material commitments—which is why the
choice is often nothing more than the reaffirmation of already existing ties. No doubt, it is also determined by the belief that we
share convictions and interests with these people, to whom we now
pledge our solidarity. But no one who has been actively engaged in
politics will believe that rational agreement or calculations of interest exhaust the idea of political commitment.

When we say that a group of this kind is worth choosing, when
we call it good, the statement can be analyzed with the terms that I
have been using: we mean, first, that the convictions expressed in its
program are rationally defensible; second, that the interests it defends ought to be defended; and third, that the feelings of sympa-
thy and affection its members express are attractive—they are feelings we already share or would like to share. The actual situation, of
course, is always more ambiguous. The group's program is a mix of
many elements, some of them more readily defensible than others.
The interests it defends, even when properly understood, often
conflict with other interests that should also be defended. The feelings of the members may include a terrible bitterness or hatred directed at political enemies, in which we may not want to join. We
have to judge the whole thing, all in all, and in the course of doing
that, we probably won't undertake the highly artificial analysis I
have just suggested, which misses the inevitable tangle of conviction and passion that shapes all our judgments. We certainly won't
be looking for groups whose members have only convictions or only
interests and no passions. There aren't any, in any case.

All this seems obvious to me, so obvious that I have been puz-
zled at many points, while writing this chapter, about how I could
say anything in conclusion that would be excitingly new or even

mildly provocative. Yet the dichotomies that set passionate intensity against some sort of interested or principled rationality, heat against light, are so pervasive in political thinking that perhaps it is enough to say simply that they are useless, that they correspond to nothing at all in the actual experience of political engagement. That isn't an argument against reason; indeed, I have tried to give reasons for making it. But it is a powerful and important corrective to liberal rationalism.

And there is a further conclusion, another correction, which I have sometimes explicitly argued for, sometimes only suggested or implied: No political party that sets itself against the established hierarchies of power and wealth, no movement for equality or national liberation, for emancipation or empowerment, will ever succeed unless it arouses the affiliative and combative passions of the people at the lower end of the hierarchies. The passions that it arouses are certain to include envy, resentment, and hatred, since these are the common consequences of hierarchical domination. They are also the emotional demons of political life, bound to call up the anxieties that are expressed in, or read into, the Donne and Yeats poems—anxieties that I assume we all share and have good reason to share. But anger at injustice and a sense of solidarity are also among the passions aroused by anti-hierarchical politics, which means that we also have good reason not to surrender too quickly to anxiety. Maybe things won't fall apart; maybe the center will hold; maybe a new center will form. Meanwhile, there is no way to join the parties and movements that are struggling for greater equality, and to support the good passions and convictions against the bad ones, except to do so . . . passionately.

CONCLUSION

Global Equality

M Y ARGUMENT HAS FOCUSED ON
domestic society—appropriately, since
liberalism is above all a domestic theory, designed to address the relationships of individuals to one another
and to the state. The justice of partic-
ular states and societies and the rights of individuals as citizens and
aliens: these are its primary concerns. But the greatest inequalities,
the most terrifying misery, the ugliest forms of human degradation
now exist in international society—which is to say, they are attrib-
utable (in part) to economic policies and practices that have global
reach, and they are measurable across state boundaries. Some countries, despite the great inequalities within them, are overwhelm-
ingly impoverished, desperately poor, while the inhabitants of others are mostly comfortable and even well-to-do.

In the aftermath of the September 11, 2001, attacks on New York and Washington, D.C., some liberal and leftist writers argued that these inequalities were the root cause of international terrorism—as if to give us a new reason for opposing them. That argument seems to me false, for both domestic and global society, because otherwise terrorism would be far more widely dispersed than it is (and far more prevalent and powerful in sub-Saharan Africa than in the Middle East). Desperate poverty makes most often for political passivity—but sometimes for opposition and revolt. When historical circumstances favor revolt, its forms are determined largely by culture and ideology, not by poverty alone or by inequality alone. Struggles for emancipation and empowerment are the most common forms of revolt, and even when the struggles are high-pitched and passionate, they don't necessarily include terrorism as one of their methods. The need to defeat terrorism is not a particularly good argument for trying to reduce inequality. There are older and better arguments, which have to do with the human suffering that unconstrained power and wealth inevitably produce. Terrorism is a different subject, and the moral and political imperatives it generates are also different. We need to address inequality in its own right, because of its immediate consequences for subordinate and impoverished individuals. So, how should we deal with the perverse effects of the global hierarchy?

The response to this question most consistent with liberal political theory is easy to describe—and a good number of liberal theorists have responded in this way. They argue that we should, right now, take whatever steps are necessary to reproduce liberalism's domestic success in the international arena. We should defend the human rights of individuals across the globe and look for international agencies that can undertake some, at least, of the functions of the liberal state: redistributing resources to enable the largest possible number of individuals to pursue happiness; sustaining a livable environment for all the world's inhabitants; maintaining a system of law enforcement aimed at equal protection for men and women, rich and poor, and so on. Liberalism's theoretical drift—even if practice lags far behind—is toward a global regime that relates directly, with equal respect and concern, to each and every human individual.[1]

A regime of this sort looks more feasible today than it did only decades ago. The development of an international version of civil society opens the way for the characteristic liberal form of mediation between individual and regime, which is the work of social movements and interest groups. Many such organizations already exist and have had some political impact, although it is hard to say how much. The most interesting feature of groups like Amnesty International, Human Rights Watch, Oxfam, Doctors Without Borders, Greenpeace, and many others, is that they recruit staff, members, and supporters across all the world's frontiers and defend the interests of men and women in many different countries.[2] Their work is not yet matched by groups aiming at economic redistribution, but after the political demonstrations in Seattle in 1999, at the World Trade Organization Ministerial Conference, it is possible to imagine a global version of social democracy: parties and unions committed to universalist principles, directing their energy, in the absence of a global state, at agencies like the WTO and the World Bank, which function in a statelike manner.

This emerging liberal politics reproduces what I have called the emancipation model at the level of international society. Amnesty International and Greenpeace are obvious examples of voluntary associations: they are the international equivalents of the American Civil Liberties Union and the Sierra Club. They act on behalf of powerless and vulnerable people. A globally effective redistributive politics would require that political parties and labor unions, which have hitherto been domestic organizations (even when they called themselves international), produce a similar equivalence, operating or cooperating across borders, looking toward a global version of countervailing power. But the unions haven't yet found international agencies that can give them the kind of support that the American state gave the CIO in the 1930s and 1940s. So far, none of the associations of the new international civil society has managed to mobilize masses of people; they are all dependent on the passionate intensity of a relatively few activists and militants. Nor is it yet clear where the political space of international civil society is located: Where might the workers of the world gather, if they were ever moved to act together? How will men and women scattered across the world's endangered environments ever find their way to a common geography and a common program? Still, global emancipation is a real politics, even if it isn't yet the work of the many.

The many are far more involved in particularist and parochial groups—among them, most importantly, nation-states and, in a few places, national liberation movements aiming at statehood. From the perspective of emancipationist politics, however, the existing states of the modern world are narrow and obstructionist organizations (and the states still to come are unlikely to be any different).[3] The advance of human rights and the success of redistribution depend on the erosion of state sovereignty, so that international labor standards, for example, or the rights of women, or the safety of ethnic and religious minorities, can be universally defined and enforced. Global emancipation *is*, in part at least, the loosening of the grip of the sovereign state on its individual members—just as domestic emancipation was, in part, the loosening of the grip of ethnic and religious communities on their members.

We have to imagine the addition of hyphenated identities, with each new one qualifying the one before: first there is a Catholic, let's say, and then a Catholic-Italian, and then a Catholic-Italian-American, and then (I have to invent a name for this last addition) a Catholic-Italian-American-Universalist. Adding *Italian* means that *Catholic* no longer tells the whole story of this person's membership and loyalty; adding *American* means that *Catholic-Italian* no longer tells the whole story, and so on. More hyphens make for more complicated and probably also freer individuals; exit from hyphenated groups and pluralized identities is easier than exit from singular groups and identities. At the end, emancipated men and women simply choose who and what they will be.

For anyone interested in greater equality, global emancipation is a necessary politics. But it can't stand by itself; its individualist and voluntarist commitments reproduce the characteristic weaknesses of domestic liberalism. It requires the same sociological sophistication and revision that I have been urging in this book. The inequalities of international society are both class/economic and categorical/political inequalities: the individual men and women who occupy the lowest ranks on the global hierarchy are there because they are poor, obviously, but also because they are (without ever having chosen to be) Congolese, Rwandan, or Bengali—or Kurdish or Palestinian. Their fate is determined by their location, by their parents, and by their nationality.

All these are factors "arbitrary from a moral point of view" according to liberal theory.[4] They shouldn't count; in a just world order, they wouldn't count. Only individual rights would count. But this argument, although it isn't exactly wrong, seems to me incomplete. Geographical location and national membership shouldn't count so long as ordinary people are denied the chance to make the best of their country and their nation. But if we ever succeed in giving them that chance, the argument about moral arbitrariness will have to be qualified. Many people in the world today are poor and powerless in part because they live in weak and dysfunctional states, which have been seized by predatory elites or warring gangs. In the most dire circumstances, in times of famine or massacre, these people may have to be rescued by foreign intervention; perhaps that is the only way to rescue them. Over the long haul, however, what they need most is an empowered and effective state. They should be helped to create such states, but the creation will ultimately have to be their own work—and this work is not arbitrary from a moral point of view. When it is done, if it is done, the children of the state-builders will be better off because of their location, their parents, and their nationality. They will be entitled to the benefits that follow from the political effort undertaken in their name, and they will be proud to claim those benefits.

The need for effective states is widely recognized in the international community, whose leaders acknowledge the necessity of "nation-building" after each local crisis (in Bosnia, Kosovo, Rwanda, and East Timor, for example)—even if most of them are unwilling to commit their own countries to the necessary expense. And nation-building is in fact state-building: it requires the creation of institutions capable of maintaining law and order, collecting taxes, providing services, and sponsoring and shaping economic activity. A good global society will have strong international regulatory agencies with the power to enforce their regulations.[5] But it will also have its own version of multiculturalism: a pluralism of states capable of delivering meat and potatoes to their citizens.

Statehood is a form of recognition—literally so: in international society we recognize states, not individuals. Stateless peoples seek that kind of recognition; it is a source of pride, and the citizens of weak states are often hungry for it, too, sensitive to any, even minor, infringements of their sovereign rights. But we should not make too much of recognition in itself, for its rewards are insufficient to the needs of the neediest people. It is better understood, in international as in domestic society, as one of the prerequisites of effective redistribution. People need states with a recognized place in the society of states. But they need strong states even more, states with relatively uncorrupted bureaucracies: these are the best recipients, and the best redistributors, of global relief and assistance. In the capitalist world economy, they can also provide some protection against freebooting speculators and ruthless entrepreneurs (although state protection will be most effective if the speculators and entrepreneurs are forced to operate within a set of international constraints). Strong states can shelter and assist infant industries; they can organize schooling and job training for citizens and workers; and they can deliver the necessary welfare services in culturally specific ways that reflect the actual pluralism of international society.

Why is this pluralism unavoidable, even morally necessary? For all the old reasons: because most men and women are attached to their political-cultural identities and loyal to the states that represent (or tolerate and protect) those identities. Most of them want to be ruled by people they can recognize as their own—who are familiar with their customary ways and common beliefs. Even the radicals and reformers among them, who are working to change some of the ways, who regularly challenge some of the beliefs, are likely to want their opposition to grow from within the community. They are still attached in this strong sense: it is their own community that they mean to reform. They will be committed to the empowerment model, as we should be, even if they/we are also emancipationists.

I think that this argument applies even to states with large national minorities and to immigrant societies where there is nothing remotely like a single set of customary ways and common beliefs. States, at their best, foster a shared political culture to which their members may be strongly attached, and they provide services for which the members may be grateful. Ethnic and religious minorities will grow accustomed even to the tensions of their coexistence, so long as they live in states that are not discriminatory and oppressive. There is no reason to think that they will regard their own state as interchangeable with all others, or its government as replaceable by some set of global bureaucrats (although they may welcome global constraints on what their state can do).

A liberal critic might interject at this point, Doesn't the sociological sophistication being recommended here involve a surrender to the most retrograde tendencies in international politics? It suggests empowering nation-states and respecting (even if we also try to modify) the sovereignty of these states—including, inevitably, the most parochial among them. It suggests de-emphasizing the search for a full-scale deliberative consensus among all the world's inhabitants and looking instead for political compromises among sovereign states and between states and civil associations and international regulatory agencies. And what would we be compromising with if not nationalist passion and religious dogma? What's so sophisticated about that? Surely it would be better to move as rapidly as possible toward a global order, a world state, capable of acting justly toward all its members, the whole human race conceived as a single community of individuals with rights.

I agree that a politics committed to working with people in states is going to encounter some nasty and repressive states, and we will have to figure out how to deal with them, much as we have to do in domestic society when we encounter chauvinist ethnic groups or fundamentalist sects. But a politics committed to transcending group life, breaking the categories of difference, is likely to be ineffective (there are many examples); and it is pretty sure to be nasty and repressive in its own way. Individuals with rights are also individuals with emotions: they have the affiliative passions that go with their practical attachments, and if we want to strengthen their hand, some of the help they need has to come via their own political associations. On the way to becoming citizens of the world, they must have an opportunity to be, and they must learn to be, competent citizens of a particular state.

So global egalitarianism requires a two-track process: first, the steady extension of international regulation, driven by the cooperative efforts of individual men and women associated to defend the environment, say, or end child labor, or alter the terms of trade, or redistribute resources; and second, the empowerment of states, driven by the demands of their own citizens for protection and welfare and funded, in critical cases (and right now there are many critical cases), by international agencies.[6] Yes, some of these demands by groups of citizens will be marked by communal fervor and will reflect its excesses; some of the empowered states will come into conflict with one another and with the newly assertive international agencies. And, yes, the resulting distributive pattern will never be fully egalitarian: it will be a mediated pattern, and the mediating agencies, the different states of the global multistate system, will be differently effective in controlling corruption, accumulating resources, sponsoring economic development, and organizing welfare services. But these are not sufficient reasons to choose an anti-state politics. What most of the world's poor most need are better states.

I suspect that liberal political theorists would have less trouble reconciling themselves to the pluralism of states if all states turned out to be liberal democracies.[7] Once again, we can best think analogously in terms of the domestic debate about multiculturalism: it would be nice if all the coexisting cultural groups were liberal, open, and non-hierarchical associations. But no genuine pluralism will ever culminate in an identity of this kind or even in a close and pervasive similarity. Pluralism makes for difference—or, conversely, it is existing differences that make pluralism necessary.

Emancipationist politics, in international as in domestic society, will press all the world's states, all the parochial associations, toward more liberal and democratic practices. This pressure will be resisted, more by some groups than by others, and the resistance will be successful here, less successful there. The states that have to be empowered won't all be as "nice" as we would like them to be. Still, citizens will be better off if their states are enabled to mobilize and distribute resources and to maintain law and order. And men and women who live in states like that are far more likely than those who live in failed states, or who are stateless, to participate in the associations of international civil society.

The empowerment and emancipation models work naturally together. Or, they work in alternation. Or, they have to be harnessed and their contradictions managed. In any case, we need them both. Considered as individual men and women, none of us are fully autonomous, and none of us are fully integrated into and bound by any of our groups. We are each unique, one and only one; and we are at the same time tied closely to specific others in ways we sometimes resist, sometimes embrace. We need a political theory, and a politics, as complicated as our own lives.

The Communitarian Critique of Liberalism

I wrote this article in 1989; it was published in *Political Theory* in February 1990 and has been reprinted many times since. Because it has played a small part in the liberalism/communitarianism debates of the past decades and is now part of the historical record of those debates, I haven't changed it in any way. The argument still seems to me basically right, although I made some revisions and, I hope, improvements in the course of developing it in the chapters of this book.

I

Intellectual fashions are notoriously short-lived, very much like fashions in popular music, art, or dress. But there are certain fashions that seem regularly to reappear. Like pleated trousers or short skirts, they are inconstant features of a larger and more steadily prevailing phenomenon—in this case, a certain way of dressing. They have brief but recurrent lives; we know their transience and expect their return. Needless to say, there is no afterlife in which trousers will be permanently pleated or skirts forever short. Recurrence is all.

Although it operates at a much higher level (an infinitely higher level?) of cultural significance, the communitarian critique of liberalism is like the pleating of trousers: transient but certain to return. It is a consistently intermittent feature of liberal politics and social organization. No liberal success will make it permanently unattractive. At the same time, no communitarian critique, however penetrating, will ever be anything more than an inconstant feature of liberalism. Someday, perhaps, there will be a larger transformation, like the shift from aristocratic knee-breeches to plebeian pants, rendering liberalism and its critics alike irrelevant. But I see no present signs of anything like that, nor am I sure that we should look forward to it. For now, there is much to be said for a recurrent critique, whose protagonists hope only for small victories, partial incorporations, and, when they are rebuffed or dismissed or coopted, fade away for a time only to return.

Communitarianism is usefully contrasted with social democracy, which has succeeded in establishing a permanent presence alongside of and sometimes conjoined with liberal politics. Social democracy has its own intermittently fashionable critics, largely anarchist and libertarian in character. Since it sponsors certain sorts of communal identification, it is less subject to criticism than liberalism is. But it can never escape such criticism entirely, for liberals and social democrats alike share a commitment to economic growth and cope (although in different ways) with the deracinated social forms that growth produces. Community itself is largely an ideological presence in modern society; it has no recurrent critics of its own. It is intermittently fashionable only because it no longer exists in anything like full strength, and it is criticized only when it is fashionable.

The communitarian critique is nonetheless a powerful one; it would not recur if it were not capable of engaging our minds and feelings. In this essay, I want to investigate the power of its current American versions and then offer a version of my own—less powerful, perhaps, than the ones with which I shall begin, but more available for incorporation within liberal (or social democratic) politics. I do not mean (I hardly have the capacity) to lay communitarianism to rest, although I would willingly wait for its reappearance in a form more coherent and incisive than that in which it currently appears. The problem with communitarian criticism today—I am not the first to notice this—is that it suggests two different, and deeply contradictory, arguments against liberalism. One of these arguments is aimed primarily at liberal practice, the other primarily at liberal theory, but they cannot both be right. It is possible that each one is partly right—indeed, I shall insist on just this partial validity—but each of the arguments is right in a way that undercuts the value of the other.

II

The first argument holds that liberal political theory accurately represents liberal social practice. As if the Marxist account of ideological reflection were literally true, and exemplified here, contemporary Western societies (American society especially) are taken to be the home of radically isolated individuals, rational egoists, and existential agents, men and women protected and divided by their inalienable rights. Liberalism tells the truth about the asocial society that liberals create—not, in fact, *ex nihilo*, as their theory suggests, but in a struggle against traditions and communities and authorities that are forgotten as soon as they are escaped, so that liberal practices seem to have no history. The struggle itself is ritually celebrated but rarely reflected on. The members of liberal society share no political or religious traditions; they can tell only one story about themselves and that is the story of *ex nihilo* creation, which begins in the state of nature or the original position. Each individual imagines himself absolutely free, unencumbered, and on his own—and enters society, accepting its obligations, only in order to minimize his risks. His goal is security, and security is, as Marx wrote, "the assurance of his egoism." And as he imagines himself, so he *really* is, "that is, an individual separated from the community, withdrawn into himself, wholly preoccupied with his private interest and acting in accordance with his private caprice. The only bond between men is natural necessity, need, and private interest."[1] (I have used masculine pronouns in order to fit my sentences to Marx's. But it is an interesting question, not addressed here, whether this first communitarian critique speaks to the experience of women: Are necessity and private interest their only bonds with one another?)

The writings of the young Marx represent one of the early appearances of communitarian criticism, and his argument, first made in the 1840s, is powerfully present today. Alasdair MacIntyre's description of the incoherence of modern intellectual and cultural life and the loss of narrative capacity makes a similar point in updated, state-of-the-art, theoretical language.[2] But the only theory that is necessary to the communitarian critique of liberalism is liberalism itself. All that the critics have to do, so they say, is to take liberal theory seriously. The self-portrait of the individual constituted only by his willfulness, liberated from all connection, without common values, binding ties, customs, or traditions—sans eyes, sans teeth, sans taste, sans everything—need only be evoked in order to be devalued: It is already the concrete absence of value. What can the real life of such a person be like? Imagine him maximizing his utilities, and society is turned into a war of all against all, the familiar rat race, in which, as Hobbes wrote, there is "no other goal, nor other garland, but being foremost."[3] Imagine him enjoying his rights, and society is reduced to the coexistence of isolated selves, for liberal rights, according to this first critique, have more to do with "exit" than with "voice."[4] They are concretely expressed in separation, divorce, withdrawal, solitude, privacy, and political apathy. And finally, the very fact that individual life can be described in these two philosophical languages, the language of utilities and the language of rights, is a further mark, says MacIntyre, of its incoherence: Men and women in liberal society no longer have access to a single moral culture within which they can learn how they ought to live.[5] There is no consensus, no public meeting-of-minds, on the nature of the good life—hence the triumph of private caprice, revealed, for example, in Sartrean existentialism, the ideological reflection of everyday capriciousness.

We liberals are free to choose, and we have a right to choose, but we have no criteria to govern our choices except our own wayward understanding of our wayward interests and desires. And so our choices lack the qualities of cohesion and consecutiveness. We can hardly remember what we did yesterday; we cannot with any assurance predict what we will do tomorrow. We cannot give a proper account of ourselves. We cannot sit together and tell comprehensible stories, and we recognize ourselves in the stories we read only when these are fragmented narratives, without plots, the literary equivalent of atonal music and nonrepresentational art.

Liberal society, seen in the light of this first communitarian critique, is fragmentation in practice; and community is the exact opposite, the home of coherence, connection, and narrative capacity. But I am less concerned here with the different accounts that might be provided of this lost Eden than I am with the repeated insistence on the reality of fragmentation after the loss. This is the common theme of all contemporary communitarianisms: neoconservative lamentation, neo-Marxist indictment, and neoclassical or republican hand-wringing. (The need for the prefix *neo* suggests again the intermittent or recurrent character of communitarian criticism.) I should think it would be an awkward theme, for if the sociological argument of liberal theory is right, if society is actually decomposed, without residue, into the problematic coexistence of individuals,

then we might well assume that liberal politics is the best way to deal
with the problems of decomposition. If we have to create an artificial and ahistorical union out of a multitude of isolated selves, why
not take the state of nature or the original position as our conceptual
starting point? Why not accept, in standard liberal fashion, the priority of procedural justice over substantive conceptions of the good,
since we can hardly expect, given our fragmentation, to agree about
the good? Michael Sandel asks whether a community of those who
put justice first can ever be more than a community of strangers.[6]
The question is a good one, but its reverse form is more immediately
relevant: If we really are a community of strangers, how can we do
anything else but put justice first?

III

We are saved from this entirely plausible line of argument by the
second communitarian critique of liberalism. The second critique
holds that liberal theory radically misrepresents real life. The world
is not like that nor could it be.

Men and women cut loose from all social ties, literally unencumbered, each one the one and only inventor of his or her own life, with
no criteria, no common standards, to guide the invention—these
are mythical figures. How can any group of people be strangers to
one another when each member of the group is born with parents,
and when these parents have friends, relatives, neighbors, comrades
at work, coreligionists, and fellow citizens—connections, in fact,
which are not so much chosen as passed on and inherited? Liberalism may well enhance the significance of purely contractual ties, but
it is obviously false to suggest, as Hobbes sometimes seemed to do,
that all our connections are mere "market friendships," voluntarist
and self-interested in character, which cannot outlast the advan-
tages they bring.[7] It is in the very nature of a human society that individuals bred within it will find themselves caught up in patterns

of relationship, networks of power, and communities of meaning. That quality of being caught up is what makes them persons of a certain sort. And only then can they make themselves persons of a (marginally) different sort by reflecting on what they are and by acting in more or less distinctive ways within the patterns, networks, and communities that are willy-nilly theirs.

The burden of the second critique is that the deep structure even of liberal society is in fact communitarian. Liberal theory distorts this reality and, insofar as we adopt the theory, deprives us of any ready access to our own experience of communal embeddedness. The rhetoric of liberalism—this is the argument of the authors of *Habits of the Heart*—limits our understanding of our own heart's habits and gives us no way to formulate the convictions that hold us together as persons and that bind persons together into a community.[8] The assumption here is that we are in fact persons and that we are in fact bound together. The liberal ideology of separatism cannot take personhood and bondedness away from us. What it does take away is the *sense* of our personhood and bondedness, and this deprivation is then reflected in liberal politics. It explains our inability to form cohesive solidarities, stable movements and parties, that might make our deep convictions visible and effective in the world. It also explains our radical dependence (brilliantly foreshadowed in Hobbes's *Leviathan*) on the central state.

But how are we to understand this extraordinary disjunction between communal experience and liberal ideology, between personal conviction and public rhetoric, and between social bondedness and political isolation? That question is not addressed by communitarian critics of the second sort. If the first critique depends on a vulgar Marxist theory of reflection, the second critique requires an equally vulgar idealism. Liberal theory now seems to have a power over and against real life that has been granted to few theories in human history. Plainly, it has not been granted to communitarian theory, which cannot, on the first argument, overcome the reality of liberal separatism and cannot, on the second argument, evoke the already existing structures of social connection. In any case, the two critical arguments are mutually inconsistent; they cannot both be true. Liberal separatism either represents or misrepresents the conditions of everyday life. It might, of course, do a little of each—the usual muddle—but that is not a satisfactory conclusion from a communitarian standpoint. For if the account of dissociation and separatism is even partly right, then we have to raise questions about the depth, so to speak, of the deep structure. And if we are all to some degree communitarians under the skin, then the portrait of social incoherence loses its critical force.

IV

But each of the two critical arguments is partly right. I will try to say what is right about each, and then ask if something plausible can be made of the parts. First, then, there cannot be much doubt that we (in the United states) live in a society where individuals are relatively dissociated and separated from one another, or better, where they are continually separating from one another—continually in motion, often in solitary and apparently random motion, as if in imitation of what physicists call Brownian movement. Hence we live in a profoundly unsettled society. We can best see the forms of unsettlement if we track the most important moves. So, consider (imitating the Chinese style) the Four Mobilities:

1. *Geographic mobility.* Americans apparently change their residence more often than any people in history, at least since the barbarian migrations, excluding only nomadic tribes and families caught up in civil or foreign wars. Moving people and their possessions from one city or town to another is a major industry in the United States, even though many people manage to move themselves. In another sense, of course, we are all self-moved, not refugees but voluntary migrants. The sense of place must be greatly

weakened by this extensive geographic mobility, although I find it hard to say whether it is superseded by mere insensitivity or by a new sense of many places. Either way, communitarian feeling seems likely to decline in importance. Communities are more than just locations, but they are most often successful when they are permanently located.

2. *Social mobility*. This article will not address the arguments about how best to describe social standing or how to measure changes, whether by income, education, class membership, or rank in the status hierarchy. It is enough to say that fewer Americans stand exactly where their parents stood or do what they did than in any society for which we have comparable knowledge. Americans may inherit many things from their parents, but the extent to which they make a different life, if only by making a different living, means that the inheritance of community, that is, the passing on of beliefs and customary ways, is uncertain at best. Whether or not children are thereby robbed of narrative capacity, they seem likely to tell different stories than their parents told.

3. *Marital mobility*. Rates of separation, divorce, and remarriage are higher today than they have ever been in our own society and probably higher than they have ever been in any other (except perhaps among Roman aristocrats, although I know of no statistics from that time, only anecdotes). The first two mobilities, geographic and social, also disrupt family life, so that siblings, for example, often live at great distances from one another, and later, as uncles and aunts, they are far removed from nephews and nieces. But what we call "broken homes" are the product of marital breaks, of husbands or wives moving out—and then, commonly, moving on to new partners. Insofar as home is the first community and the first school of ethnic identity and religious conviction, this kind of breakage must have countercommunitarian consequences. It means that children often do not hear continuous or identical stories from the adults with whom they live. (Did the greater number of children

ever hear such stories? The death of one spouse and the remarriage of the other may have once been as common as divorce and remarriage are today. But, then, other sorts of mobility have to be considered: Both men and women are more likely today to marry across class, ethnic, and religious lines; remarriage will therefore often produce extraordinarily complex and socially diverse families—which probably are without historical precedent.)

4. *Political mobility*. Loyalty to leaders, movements, parties, clubs, and urban machines seems to decline rapidly as place and social standing and family membership become less central in the shaping of personal identity. Liberal citizens stand outside all political organizations and then choose the one that best serves their ideals or interests. They are, ideally, independent voters, that is, people who move around; they choose for themselves rather than voting as their parents did, and they choose freshly each time rather than repeating themselves. As their numbers increase, they make for a volatile electorate and hence for institutional instability, particularly at the local level where political organization once served to reinforce communal ties.

The effects of the Four Mobilities are intensified in a variety of ways by other social developments which we are likely to talk about in the common metaphor of movement: the advance of knowledge, technological progress, and so on. But I am concerned here only with the actual movement of individuals. Liberalism is, most simply, the theoretical endorsement and justification of this movement.[9] In the liberal view, then, the Four Mobilities represent the enactment of liberty and the pursuit of (private or personal) happiness. And it has to be said that, conceived in this way, liberalism is a genuinely popular creed. Any effort to curtail mobility in the four areas described here would require a massive and harsh application of state power. Nevertheless, this popularity has an underside of sadness and discontent that are intermittently articulated, and communitarianism is, most simply, the intermittent articulation of these feelings. It reflects a sense of loss, and the loss is real. People do not always leave their old neighborhoods or hometowns willingly or happily. Moving may be a personal adventure in our standard cultural mythologies, but it is as often a family trauma in real life. The same thing is true of social mobility, which carries people down as well as up and requires adjustments that are never easy to manage. Marital breaks may sometimes give rise to new and stronger unions, but they also pile up what we might think of as family fragments: single-parent households, separated and lonely men and women, and abandoned children. And independence in politics is often a not-so-splendid isolation: Individuals with opinions are cut loose from groups with programs. The result is a decline in "the sense of efficacy," with accompanying effects on commitment and morale.

All in all, we liberals probably know one another less well, and with less assurance, than people once did, although we may see more aspects of the other than they saw, and recognize in him or her a wider range of possibilities (including the possibility of moving on). We are more often alone than people once were, being without neighbors we can count on, relatives who live nearby or with whom we are close, or comrades at work or in the movement. That is the truth of the first communitarian argument. We must now fix the limits of this truth by seeking what is true in the second argument.

In its easiest version, the second argument—that we are really, at bottom, creatures of community—is certainly true but of uncertain significance. The ties of place, class or status, family, and even politics survive the Four Mobilities to a remarkable extent. To take just one example, from the last of the Four: It remains true, even today in this most liberal and mobile of societies, that the best predictor of how people will vote is our knowledge of how their parents voted.[10] All those dutifully imitative young Republicans and Democrats testify to the failure of liberalism to make independence or waywardness of mind the distinctive mark of its adherents. The predictive value of parental behavior holds even for independent voters: They are simply the heirs of independence. But we do not know to what extent inheritances of this sort are a dwindling communal resource; it may be that each generation passes on less than it received. The full liberalization of the social order, the production and reproduction of self-inventing individuals, may take a long time, much longer, indeed, than liberals themselves expected. There is not much comfort here for communitarian critics, however; while they can recognize and value the survival of older ways of life, they cannot count on, and they must have anxieties about, the vitality of those ways.

But there is another approach to the truth of the second critical argument. Whatever the extent of the Four Mobilities, they do not seem to move us so far apart that we can no longer talk with one another. We often disagree, of course, but we disagree in mutually comprehensible ways. I should think it fairly obvious that the philosophical controversies that MacIntyre laments are not in fact a mark of social incoherence. Where there are philosophers, there will be controversies, just as where there are knights, there will be tournaments. But these are highly ritualized activities, which bear witness to the connection, not the disconnection, of their protagonists. Even political conflict in liberal societies rarely takes forms so extreme as to set its protagonists beyond negotiation and compromise, procedural justice, and the very possibility of speech. The American civil rights struggle is a nice example of a conflict for which our moral/political language was and is entirely adequate. The fact that the struggle has had only partial success does not reflect linguistic inadequacy but rather political failures and defeats.

Martin Luther King, Jr.'s speeches evoked a palpable tradition, a set of common values, such that public disagreement could focus only on how (or how quickly) they might best be realized.[11] But this is not, so to speak, a traditionalist tradition, a *Gemeinschaft* tradition, a survival of the preliberal past. It is a liberal tradition modified, no doubt, by survivals of different sorts. The modifications are most obviously Protestant and republican in character, though by no means exclusively so. The years of mass immigration have brought a great variety of ethnic and religious memories to bear on American politics. What all of them bear on, however, is liberalism. The language of individual rights—voluntary association, pluralism, toleration, separation, privacy, free speech, the career open to talents, and so on—is simply inescapable. Who among us seriously attempts to escape? If we really are situated selves, as the second communitarian critique holds, then our situation is largely captured by that vocabulary. This is the truth of the second critique. Does it make any sense, then, to argue that liberalism prevents us from understanding or maintaining the ties that bind us together?

It makes some sense, because liberalism is a strange doctrine, which seems continually to undercut itself, to disdain its own traditions, and to produce in each generation renewed hopes for a more absolute freedom from history and society alike. Much of liberal political theory, from Locke to Rawls, is an effort to fix and stabilize the doctrine in order to end the endlessness of liberal liberation. But beyond every current version of liberalism, there is always a super liberalism, which, as Roberto Unger says of his own doctrine, "pushes the liberal premises about state and society, about freedom from dependence and governance of social relations by the will, to the point at which they merge into a large ambition: the building of a social world less alien to a self that can always violate the generative rules of its own mental or social constructs."[12] Although Unger was once identified as a communitarian, this ambition—large indeed!—seems designed to prevent not only any stabilization of liberal doctrine but also any recovery or creation of community. For there is no imaginable community that would not be alien to the eternally transgressive self. If the ties that bind us together do not *bind* us, there can be no such thing as community. If it is anything at all, communitarianism is antithetical to transgression.

And the transgressive self is antithetical even to the liberal community which is its creator and sponsor.[13]

Liberalism is a self-subverting doctrine; for that reason, it really does require periodic communitarian correction. But it is not a particularly helpful form of correction to suggest that liberalism is literally incoherent or that it can be replaced by some preliberal or antiliberal community waiting somehow just beneath the surface or just beyond the horizon. Nothing is waiting; American communitarians have to recognize that there is no one out there but separated, rights-bearing, voluntarily associating, freely speaking, liberal selves. It would be a good thing, though, if we could teach those selves to know themselves as social beings, the historical products of, and in part the embodiments of, liberal values. For the communitarian correction of liberalism cannot be anything other than a selective reinforcement of those same values or, to appropriate the well-known phrase of Michael Oakeshott, a pursuit of the intimations of community within them.

V

The place to begin the pursuit is with the liberal idea of voluntary association, which is not well understood, it seems to me, either among liberals or among their communitarian critics. In both its theory and its practice, liberalism expresses strong associative tendencies alongside its dissociative tendencies: Its protagonists form groups as well as split off from the groups they form; they join up and resign, marry and divorce. Nevertheless, it is a mistake, and a characteristically liberal mistake, to think that the existing patterns of association are entirely or even largely voluntary and contractual, that is, the product of will alone. In a liberal society, as in every other society, people are born into very important sorts of groups, born with identities, male or female, for example, working class, Catholic or Jewish, black, Democrat, and so on. Many of their subsequent associations (like their subsequent careers) merely express these underlying identities, which, again, are not so much chosen as enacted.[14] Liberalism is distinguished less by the freedom to form groups on the basis of these identities than by the freedom to leave the groups and sometimes even the identities behind. Association is always at risk in a liberal society. The boundaries of the group are not policed; people come and go, or they just fade into the distance without ever quite acknowledging that they have left. That is why liberalism is plagued by free-rider problems—by people who continue to enjoy the benefits of membership and identity while no longer participating in the activities that produce those benefits.[15] Communitarianism, by contrast, is the dream of a perfect free-riderlessness.

At its best, the liberal society is the "social union of social unions" that John Rawls described: a pluralism of groups bonded by shared ideas of toleration and democracy.[16] But if all the groups are precarious, continually on the brink of dissolution or abandonment, then the larger union must also be weak and vulnerable. Or, alternatively, its leaders and officials will be driven to compensate for the failures of association elsewhere by strengthening their own union, that is, the central state, beyond the limits that liberalism has established. These limits are best expressed in terms of individual rights and civil liberties, but they also include a prescription for state neutrality. The good life is pursued by individuals, sponsored by groups; the state presides over the pursuit and the sponsorship but does not participate in either. Presiding is singular in character; pursuing and sponsoring are plural. Hence it is a critical question for liberal theory and practice whether the associative passions and energies of ordinary people are likely over the long haul to survive the Four Mobilities and prove themselves sufficient to the requirements of pluralism. There is at least some evidence that they will not prove sufficient—without a little help. But, to repeat an old question, whence cometh our help? A few of the existing social unions live in the expectation of divine assistance. For the rest, we can only help one another, and the agency through which help of that sort comes most expeditiously is the state. But what kind of state is it that fosters associative activities? What kind of a social union is it that includes without incorporating a great and discordant variety of social unions?

Obviously, it is a liberal state and social union; any other kind is too dangerous for communities and individuals alike. It would be an odd enterprise to argue in the name of communitarianism for an alternative state, for that would be to argue against our own political traditions and to repudiate whatever community we already have. But the communitarian correction does require a liberal state of a certain sort, conceptually though not historically unusual: a state that is, at least over some part of the terrain of sovereignty, deliberately nonneutral. The standard liberal argument for neutrality is an induction from social fragmentation. Since dissociated individuals will never agree on the good life, the state must allow them to live as they think best, subject only to John Stuart Mill's harm principle, without endorsing or sponsoring any particular understanding of what "best" means. But there is a problem here: The more dissociated individuals are, the stronger the state is likely to be, since it will be the only or the most important social union. And then membership in the state, the only good that is shared by all individuals, may well come to seem the good that is "best."

There is only to repeat the first communitarian critique, and it invites a response like the second critique: that the state is not in fact the only or even, for ordinary people in their everyday lives, the most important social union. All sorts of other groups continue to exist and to give shape and purpose to the lives of their members, despite the triumph of individual rights, the Four Mobilities in which that triumph is manifest, and the free-riding that it makes possible. But these groups are continually at risk. And so the state, if it is to remain a liberal state, must endorse and sponsor some of them, namely, those that seem most likely to provide shapes and purposes congenial to the shared values of a liberal society.[17] No doubt, there are problems here too, and I do not mean to deny their difficulty. But I see no way to avoid some such formulation—and not only for theoretical reasons. The actual history of the best liberal states, as of the best social democratic states (and these tend increasingly to be the same states), suggests that they behave in exactly this way, although often very inadequately.

Let me give three relatively familiar examples of state behavior of this kind. First, the Wagner Act of the 1930s: This was not a standard liberal law, hindering the hindrances to union organization, for it actively fostered union organization, and it did so precisely by solving the free-rider problem. By requiring collective bargaining whenever there was majority support (but not necessarily unanimous support) for the union, and then by allowing union shops, the Wagner Act sponsored the creation of strong unions capable, at least to some degree, of determining the shape of industrial relations.[18] Of course, there could not be strong unions without working-class solidarity; unionization is parasitic on underlying communities of feeling and belief. But those underlying communities were already being eroded by the Four Mobilities when the Wagner Act was passed, and so the act served to counter the dissociative tendencies of liberal society. It was nevertheless a liberal law, for the unions that it helped create enhanced the lives of individual workers and were subject to dissolution and abandonment in accordance with liberal principles should they ever cease to do that.

The second example is the use of tax exemptions and matching grants of tax money to enable different religious groups to run extensive systems of day-care centers, nursing homes, hospitals, and so on—welfare societies inside the welfare state. I do not pretend that these private and pluralist societies compensate for the shoddiness of the American welfare state. But they do improve the delivery of services by making it a more immediate function of communal solidarity. The state's role here, besides establishing minimal standards, is to abate, since in this case it cannot entirely solve, the free-rider problem. If some number of men and women end up in a Catholic nursing home, even though they never contributed to a Catholic charity, they will at least have paid their taxes. But why not nationalize the entire welfare system and end free-ridership? The liberal response is that the social union of social unions must always operate at two levels: A welfare system run entirely by private, nonprofit associations would be dangerously inadequate and inequitable in its coverage; and a totally nationalized system would deny expression to local and particularist solidarities.[19]

The third example is the passage of plant-closing laws designed to afford some protection to local communities of work and residence. Inhabitants are insulated, though only for a time, against market pressure to move out of their old neighborhoods and search for work elsewhere. Although the market "needs" a highly mobile work force, the state takes other needs into account, not only in a welfarist way (through unemployment insurance and job retraining programs) but also in a communitarian way. But the state is not similarly committed to the preservation of every neighborhood community. It is entirely neutral toward communities of ethnicity and residence, offering no protection against strangers who want to move in. Here, geographic mobility remains a positive value, one of the rights of citizens.

Unions, religious organizations, and neighborhoods each draw on feelings and beliefs that, in principle if not always in history, predate the emergence of the liberal state. How strong these feelings and beliefs are, and what their survival value is, I cannot say. Have the unions established such a grip on the imaginations of their members as to make for good stories? There are some good stories, first told, then retold, and sometimes even re-enacted. But the narrative line does not seem sufficiently compelling to younger workers to sustain anything like the old working-class solidarity. Nor is it sufficient for a religious organization to provide life-cycle services for its members if they are no longer interested in religious services. Nor are neighborhoods proof for long against market pressure. Still, communal feeling and belief seem considerably more stable than we once thought they would be, and the proliferation of secondary associations in liberal society is remarkable—even if many of them have short lives and transient memberships. One has a sense of people working together and trying to cope, and not, as the first communitarian critique suggests, just getting by on their own, by themselves, one by one.

VI

A good liberal (or social democratic) state enhances the possibilities for cooperative coping. John Dewey provided a useful account of such a state in *The Public and Its Problems*. Published in 1927, the book is a commentary on and partial endorsement of an earlier round of communitarian criticism. Dewey shared with the critics of his time, who called themselves "pluralists," an uneasiness with the sovereign state, but he was not quite as uneasy as most of them were. He also shared an admiration for what he called "primary groupings" within the state, but he was more inclined than the pluralists were to qualify his admiration. Primary groupings, he wrote, are "good, bad, and indifferent," and they cannot by their mere existence fix the limits of state activity. The state is not "only an umpire to avert and remedy trespasses of one group upon another." It has a larger function: "It renders the desirable association solider and more coherent. . . . It places a discount upon injurious groupings and renders their tenure of life precarious . . . [and] it gives the individual members of valued associations greater liberty and security; it relieves them of hampering conditions. . . . It enables individual members to count with reasonable certainty upon what others will do."[20] These may seem like tasks too extensive for

a *liberal* state, but they are constrained by the constitutional establishment of individual rights—which are themselves (on the prag-
matic understanding) not so much recognitions of what individuals
by nature are or have as expressions of hope about what they will be
and do. Unless individuals act together in certain ways, state action
of the sort that Dewey recommended cannot get started. When we
recognize the "right of the citizens peacefully to assemble," for example, we are hoping for assemblies of citizens. If we then discrim-
inate among such assemblies, we do so on limited grounds, fostering only those that really do express communities of feeling and
belief and do not violate liberal principles of association.

It is often argued these days that the nonneutral state, whose activities I have made some attempt to justify, is best understood in republican terms. A revival of neoclassical republicanism provides
much of the substance of contemporary communitarian politics.
The revival, I have to say, is largely academic; unlike other versions
of communitarianism in Dewey's time and ours, it has no external
reference. There really are unions, churches, and neighborhoods in
American society, but there are virtually no examples of republican
association and no movement or party aimed at promoting such association. Dewey would probably not recognize his "public," nor
Rawls his "social union," as a version of republicanism, if only because in both these cases, energy and commitment have been
drained from the singular and narrowly political association to the
more various associations of civil society. Republicanism, by contrast, is an integrated and unitary doctrine in which energy and
commitment are focused primarily on the political realm. It is a doctrine adapted (in both its classical and neoclassical forms) to the
needs of small, homogeneous communities, where civil society is
radically undifferentiated. Perhaps the doctrine can be extended to
account for a "republic of republics," a decentralized and participatory revision of liberal democracy. A considerable strengthening of
local governments would then be required in the hope of encourag-

ing the development and display of civic virtue in a pluralist variety of social settings. This indeed is a pursuit of the intimations of community *within* liberalism, for it has more to do with John Stuart Mill than with Rousseau. Now we are to imagine the nonneutral state empowering cities, towns, and boroughs; fostering neighborhood committees and review boards; and always on the lookout for bands of citizens ready to take responsibility for local affairs.[21]

None of this is any guarantee against the erosion of the underlying communities or the death of local loyalties. It is a matter of principle that communities must always be at risk. And the great paradox of a liberal society is that one cannot set oneself against this principle without also setting oneself against the traditional practices and shared understandings of the society. Here, respect for tradition requires the precariousness of traditionalism. If the first communitarian critique were true in its entirety, if there were no communities and no traditions, then we could just proceed to invent new ones. Insofar as the second critique is even partly true, and the work of communal invention is well begun and continually in progress, we must rest content with the kinds of corrections and enhancements—they would be, in fact, more radical than these terms suggest—that Dewey described.

VII

I have avoided until now what is often taken to be the central issue between liberals and their communitarian critics—the constitution of the self.[22] Liberalism, it is commonly said, is founded on the idea of a presocial self, a solitary and sometimes heroic individual confronting society, who is fully formed before the confrontation begins. Communitarian critics then argue, first, that instability and dissociation are the actual and disheartening achievement of individuals of this sort and, second, that there really cannot be individuals of this sort. The critics are commonly said in turn to believe in a radically socialized self that can never "confront" society because it is, from the beginning, entangled in society, itself the embodiment of social values. The disagreement seems sharp enough, but in fact, in practice, it is not sharp at all—for neither of these views can be sustained for long by anyone who goes beyond staking out a position and tries to elaborate an argument.[23] Nor does liberal or communitarian theory require views of this sort. Contemporary liberals are not committed to a presocial self, but only to a self capable of reflecting critically on the values that have governed its socialization; and communitarian critics, who are doing exactly that, can hardly go on to claim that socialization is everything. The philosophical and psychological issues here go very deep, but so far as politics is concerned, there is little to be won on this battlefield; concessions from the other side come too easily to count as victories.

The central issue for political theory is not the constitution of the self but the connection of constituted selves, the pattern of social relations. Liberalism is best understood as a theory of relationship, which has voluntary association at its center and which understands voluntariness as the right of rupture or withdrawal. What makes a marriage voluntary is the permanent possibility of divorce. What makes any identity or affiliation voluntary is the easy availability of alternative identities and affiliations. But the easier this easiness is, the less stable all our relationships are likely to become. The Four Mobilities take hold and society seems to be in perpetual motion, so that the actual subject of liberal practice, it might be said, is not a presocial but a postsocial self, free at last from all but the most temporary and limited alliances. Now, the liberal self reflects the fragmentation of liberal society: It is radically undetermined and divided, forced to invent itself anew for every public occasion. Some liberals celebrate this freedom and self-invention; all communitarians lament its arrival, even while insisting that it is not a possible human condition.

I have argued that insofar as liberalism tends toward instability and dissociation, it requires periodic communitarian correction. Rawls's "social union of social unions" reflects and builds on an earlier correction of this kind, the work of American writers like Dewey, Randolph Bourne, and Horace Kallen. Rawls has given us a generalized version of Kallen's argument that America, after the great immigration, was and should remain a "nation of nationalities."[24] In fact, however, the erosion of nationality seems to be a feature of liberal social life, despite intermittent ethnic revivals like that of the late 1960s and 1970s. We can generalize from this to the more or less steady attenuation of all the underlying bonds that make social unions possible. There is no strong or permanent remedy for communal attenuation short of an antiliberal curtailment of the Four Mobilities and the rights of rupture and divorce on which they rest. Communitarians sometimes dream of such a curtailment, but they rarely advocate it. The only community that most of them actually know, after all, is just this liberal union of unions, always precarious and always at risk. They cannot triumph over this liberalism; they can only, sometimes, reinforce its internal associative capacities. The reinforcement is only temporary, because the capacity for dissociation is also strongly internalized and highly valued. That is why communitarianism criticism is doomed—it probably is not a terrible fate—to eternal recurrence.

Acknowledgments

Chapters 1, 2, and 6 were originally presented as the Max Horkheimer Lectures at the Johann Wolfgang Goethe University in Frankfurt, Germany, and were published in German by Fischer Tashenbuch Verlag under the title *Vernuft, Politik und Leidenschaft* in 1999. An early version of Chapter 3 was given as a lecture at Tel Hai Academic College in Israel and was published in Hebrew in a collection edited by Ohad Nachtomy: *Multiculturalism in the Israeli Context* (Jerusalem: Magnes Press, 2003); a rewritten and much longer version appeared in *Forms of Justice: Critical Perspectives on David Miller's Political Philosophy*, edited by Daniel A. Bell and Avner de-Shalit (Lanham, Md.: Rowman and Littlefield, 2003). Chapter 4 was originally written for an Ethikon Institute conference and was published in *Alternative Conceptions of Civil Society*, edited by Simone Chambers and Will Kymlicka (Princeton: Princeton University Press, 2002). Chapter 5 also appeared in a collection of essays on Amy Gutmann and Dennis Thompson's *Democracy and Disagreement,* in a book called *Deliberative Politics,* edited by Stephen Macedo (New York: Oxford University Press, 1999). A version of Chapter 6 appeared in *Philosophy and Social Criticism* 28, no. 6 (2002). All these pieces have been substantially revised for this book—with help from Yale University Press's anonymous readers; I am especially grateful to reader number three.

In the course of writing and rewriting these chapters, I have benefited from the comments and criticism of many people. I can list only some of them here: Iring Fetscher, Axel Honneth, Mathias Lutz-Bachmann, Lutz Wingert, and Ruth Zimmerling, all of whom were present at the Horkheimer lectures; and, on this side of the Atlantic, Ronald Beiner, Seyla Benhabib, Amy Gutmann, Will Kymlicka, Clifford Orwin, Dennis Thompson, and my colleagues at the Institute for Advanced Study, Clifford Geertz, Joan Scott, Eric Maskin. There are a few more friends who haven't knowingly had a hand here but whose writings have significantly influenced my arguments: George Kateb, David Miller, Susan Moller Okin, Thomas Pogge, and Iris Marion Young.

I am grateful to my secretary, Ame Dyckman, who helped me navigate my computer's insanities and who put all the pieces of this book together in the form required by the publisher.

Larisa Heimert of Yale University Press was determined that my Horkheimer lectures should be turned into an American book; she is not responsible, however, for how the book turned out. Mary Pasti, once again, provided wonderfully gentle, firm, and skillful editorial guidance.

I have dedicated this book to my grandchildren, in the hope that they will live in a more strongly liberal, democratic, and egalitarian America.

Notes

Introduction

1. See my "Communitarian Critique of Liberalism," *Political Theory* 18, no. 1 (February 1990): 6–23, reprinted without revision as an appendix to this book.

2. See, for example, Nancy L. Rosenblum, *Membership and Morals: The Personal Uses of Pluralism in America* (Princeton: Princeton University Press, 1998); Jeff Spinner-Halev, *Surviving Diversity: Religion and Democratic Citizenship* (Baltimore: Johns Hopkins University Press, 2000); Jacob T. Levy, *The Multiculturalism of Fear* (Oxford: Oxford University Press, 2000); and Amy Gutmann, *Identity in Democracy* (Princeton: Princeton University Press, 2003).

3. For a careful refutation of the first of these charges, see Keith Banting and Will Kymlicka, "Are Multiculturalist Policies Bad for the Welfare State?" *Dissent* (Fall 2003): 59–66.

4. Will Kymlicka, *Liberalism, Community, and Culture* (Oxford: Oxford University Press, 1989); Susan Moller Okin (with respondents), *Is Multiculturalism Bad for Women?* ed. Joshua Cohen, Matthew Howard, and Martha Nussbaum (Princeton: Princeton University Press, 1999).

5. See, for example, Andrew Koppelman, *Antidiscrimination Law and Social Equality* (New Haven: Yale University Press, 1996); and Ayelet Shachar,

Multicultural Jurisdictions: Cultural Differences and Women's Rights (Cambridge: Cambridge University Press, 2001).

CHAPTER ONE. *Involuntary Association*

1. In the first incarnation of this essay, I wrote only of escape. That this is insufficient is persuasively argued in Susan Moller Okin's essay " 'Mistresses of Their Own Destiny': Group Rights, Gender, and Realistic Rights of Exit," *Ethics* 112, no. 2 (January 2002): 205–230. Egalitarian politics requires at least the possibility of internal opposition.

2. Jean-Jacques Rousseau, *The Social Contract*, trans. G. D. H. Cole (New York: E. P. Dutton, Everyman's Library, 1950), book I, chap. 1, pp. 3–4.

3. See A. Campbell et al., *The American Voter* (New York: Wiley, 1960), pp. 147–148.

4. Helpful also to democratic politics: this is the argument of A. D. Lindsay in *The Modern Democratic State* (London: Oxford University Press, 1943), chap. 3.

5. On Abraham, see Louis Ginzberg, *The Legends of the Jews*, trans. Henrietta Szold (Philadelphia: Jewish Publication Society, 1961), I: 213–214. On Bunyan's Christian, see *The Pilgrim's Progress* (New York: New American Library, 1964), p. 19 ("The Second Part," starting on p. 151, is the sequel).

6. Consider the remarkable *Robert's Rules of Order*, which is often invoked in the internal debates of the most radical associations, pledged to newness everywhere else.

7. Also before they are objects of reflection: the Abraham story was first told long after the establishment of the covenanted people it is meant to explain and legitimate. John Bunyan wrote at the end of a century of experiment with the "gathered congregation."

8. See my *Obligations: Essays on Disobedience, War, and Citizenship* (Cambridge, Mass.: Harvard University Press, 1970), esp. the fifth essay. See also A. John Simmons, *Moral Principles and Political Obligation* (Princeton: Princeton University Press, 1979).

9. At least, they are justified subject to democratic conditions, like those provided in the Wagner Act: crucially, that the closed shop is agreed to by an uncoerced majority of the workers. See Irving Bernstein, *A History of the American Worker, 1933–1941: Turbulent Years* (Boston: Houghton Mifflin, 1970), pp. 327–328. For a theoretical defense of the union shop, see Stuart White, "Trade Unionism in a Liberal State," in Amy Gutmann, ed., *Freedom of Association* (Princeton: Princeton University Press, 1998), chap. 12.

10. One qualification here: in many political communities, it is possible to be a permanent resident alien, but this also is a fixed status with rights and obligations. Conceivably, as I have argued elsewhere, one should be allowed to

choose alienship or citizenship, but one can't choose the concomitant rights and obligations; see my essay "Political Alienation and Military Service," in Walzer, *Obligations,* chap. 5.

11. Rousseau, *Social Contract,* book III, chap. 18. Cf. "The Obligations of Oppressed Minorities," in Walzer, *Obligations,* chap. 3.

12. The fundamental principle of responsibility is first established in the Babylonian Talmud, tractate Shabbat, 54b.

13. Nancy J. Hirschmann, "Eastern Veiling, Western Freedom?" *Review of Politics* 59, no. 3 (Summer 1997): 461–488.

14. Iring Fetscher, *Arbeit und Spiel* (Stuttgart: Phillip Reclam, Jun., 1983), pp. 164–165.

15. Julia Kristeva, *Nations Without Nationalism,* trans. Leon Roudiez (New York: Columbia University Press, 1993), p. 35.

16. George Kateb, "Notes on Pluralism," *Social Research* 61, no. 3 (Fall 1994): 531.

17. Harold Rosenberg, *The Tradition of the New* (New York: Horizon Press, 1959): the phrase is the title of part IV.

CHAPTER TWO. *The Collectivism of Powerlessness*

1. See Alexander Hamilton, John Jay, and James Madison, *The Federalist* (New York: Modern Library, n.d.), esp. no. 51, pp. 335–341.

2. Jean-Jacques Rousseau, *The Social Contract,* trans. G. D. H. Cole (New York: E. P. Dutton, Everyman's Library, 1950), book III, chap. 1, pp. 54–60.

3. In describing this debate I have drawn most importantly on C. Wright Mills, *The Power Elite* (New York: Oxford University Press, 1956); Robert A. Dahl, *Who Governs? Democracy and Power in an American City* (New Haven: Yale University Press, 1961); Steven Lukes, *Power: A Radical View* (London: Macmillan, 1974); Dennis H. Wrong, *Power: Its Forms, Bases, and Uses* (New York: Harper and Row, 1980); and Jeffrey C. Isaac, *Power and Marxist Theory: A Realist View* (Ithaca: Cornell University Press, 1987). But since I lived through these debates, I am probably also remembering arguments whose sources I have forgotten.

4. Peter Bachrach and Morton S. Baratz, "The Two Faces of Power," *American Political Science Review* 56 (November 1962): 947–952.

5. John Kenneth Galbraith, *American Capitalism: The Concept of Countervailing Power* (Boston: Houghton Mifflin, 1952).

6. For a personal account of what these changes were like in the steel industry, see Jack Metzgar, *Striking Steel: Solidarity Remembered* (Philadelphia: Temple University Press, 2000).

7. Charles Tilly, *Durable Inequality* (Berkeley: University of California Press, 1998).

8. For a description of black Americans along these lines, see Glenn C. Loury, *The Anatomy of Racial Inequality* (Cambridge, Mass.: Harvard University Press, 2002).

9. Alistair Horne, *A Savage War of Peace: Algeria, 1954–1962* (New York: Viking, 1977), chaps. 1–3; p. 43 for the offer of equal rights.

10. For a more optimistic view of the French capacity to create an egalitarian pluralism, see Pierre Birnbaum, *The Idea of France*, trans. M. B. De-Bevoise (New York: Hill and Wang, 2001).

11. These arguments appear not only in everyday (male) political thinking but also in high theory: see Susan Moller Okin, *Women in Western Political Thought* (Princeton: Princeton University Press, 1979); and Jean Bethke Elshtain, *Public Man, Private Woman: Women in Social and Political Thought* (Princeton: Princeton University Press, 1981).

12. Jane J. Mansbridge, in *Why We Lost the ERA* (Chicago: University of Chicago Press, 1986), provides an example of a failed campaign but one that perfectly illustrates the emancipation model.

13. Jon Elster, *Ulysses and the Sirens: Studies in Rationality and Irrationality* (Cambridge: Cambridge University Press, 1979).

14. I draw here on some arguments that I first made in "Multiculturalism and the Politics of Interest," in David Biale, Michael Galchinsky, and Susannah Heschel, eds., *Insider/Outsider: American Jews and Multiculturalism* (Berkeley: University of California Press, 1998), pp. 88–98.

15. For an argument that runs parallel to my own on these questions, see David Carroll Cochran, *The Color of Freedom: Race and Contemporary American Liberalism* (Albany: State University of New York Press, 1999).

16. Arthur M. Schlesinger, Jr., *The Disuniting of America* (New York: Norton, 1992).

Chapter Three. *Cultural Rights*

1. For arguments with which I am generally sympathetic, see Will Kymlicka, *Liberalism, Community, and Culture* (Oxford: Oxford University Press, 1989); Kymlicka, *Multicultural Citizenship* (Oxford: Clarendon Press, 1996); and Charles Taylor, *Multiculturalism and "The Politics of Recognition,"* ed. Amy Gutmann (Princeton: Princeton University Press, 1992). For the full range of views, see Kymlicka, ed., *The Rights of Minority Cultures* (Oxford: Oxford University Press, 1995).

2. On the character of ethnic and religious communities in the United States, see my *What It Means to Be an American* (New York: Marsilio, 1992).

3. David Miller, *On Nationality* (Oxford: Clarendon Press, 1995), p. 144.

4. Lewis A. Coser, *Greedy Institutions: Patterns of Undivided Commitment* (New York: Free Press, 1974).

5. On the necessary content of an education in democratic values, see Amy Gutmann, *Democratic Education* (Princeton: Princeton University Press, 1987). The revised edition, published in 1999, has an epilogue that directly addresses the issues discussed here.

6. For a strong argument on this and related issues, see Susan Moller Okin, "Feminism and Multiculturalism: Some Tensions," in Dan Avnon and Avner de-Shalit, eds., *Liberalism and Its Practice* (London: Routledge, 1999), pp. 81-105. See also Anne Phillips, "Democracy and Difference: Some Problems for Feminist Theory," in Kymlicka, ed., *Rights of Minority Cultures,* pp. 288-299.

7. Many different possibilities are considered in the articles collected in Yael Tamir, ed., *Democratic Education in a Multicultural State* (Oxford: Blackwell, 1995).

8. For an example of a strongly interventionist liberalism, see Stephen Macedo, *Diversity and Distrust: Civic Education in a Multicultural Society* (Cambridge, Mass.: Harvard University Press, 2000). My own dilemma might best be described this way: I am looking for a position between that of Moshe Halbertal and Avishai Margalit, who, in "Liberalism and the Right to Culture," *Social Research* 61, no. 3 (1994): 491, claim that democratic states sometimes have "an obligation to support cultures that flout the rights of the individual," and the position of Amy Gutmann, who, in *Identity in Democracy* (Princeton: Princeton University Press, 2003), p. 51, argues that democratic states must always "respect individuals as . . . purposive agents with equal freedom to live their lives as they see fit." But perhaps there is no viable space between those positions.

9. Jean-Jacques Rousseau, *The Social Contract,* trans. G. D. H. Cole (New York: E. P. Dutton, Everyman's Library, 1950), book I, chap. 8, p. 19: "obedience to a law which we prescribe to ourselves is liberty."

10. Miller, *On Nationality,* p. 145.

11. David Miller, *Citizenship and National Identity* (Cambridge: Polity, 2000), p. 57.

CHAPTER FOUR. *Civil Society and the State*

1. In modern societies, marriage itself is a voluntary association, even if it entangles the partners with relatives they have not chosen and responsibilities they may not yet understand. And people do walk away from their families. For these reasons, and also for the feminist reasons suggested by Anne Phillips in her essay "Does Feminism Need a Conception of Civil Society?" in Simone Chambers and Will Kymlicka, eds., *Alternative Conceptions of Civil Society* (Princeton: Princeton University Press, 2002), pp. 71-89, it might be better to include families in our account of civil society. On balance, I think

that the special intimacies of familial life set it apart, but I argue below for including family-like groups—ethnic and religious communities.

2. For a useful but perhaps too complicated account of the relation of civil society to "economic society," see Jean L. Cohen and Andrew Arato, *Civil Society and Political Theory* (Cambridge, Mass.: MIT Press, 1992), pp. 75–82 (page 74 for the standard anti-statism of civil society theory). Also see Loren Lomasky, "Classical Liberalism and Civil Society," in Chambers and Kymlicka, eds., *Alternative Conceptions*, pp. 90–112.

3. For an account of Jean-Paul Sartre's idea of seriality, more accessible than his own, see R. D. Laing and D. G. Cooper, *Reason and Violence: A Decade of Sartre's Philosophy, 1950–1960* (New York: Pantheon, 1971), pp. 121ff. A serial group is a "plurality of [individual] solitudes." I am imagining civil society as a plurality of collective solitudes, in which case liberal pluralism doesn't work—for reasons ably canvassed in Adam Seligman, *The Idea of Civil Society* (New York: Free Press, 1992), esp. chap. 4.

4. Sheri Berman, "Civil Society and the Collapse of the Weimar Republic," *World Politics* (April 1997): 401–429; Lewis A. Coser, *Greedy Institutions: Patterns of Undivided Commitment* (New York: Free Press, 1974).

5. For a fuller and theoretically specific list of the values of civil society, see Jean L. Cohen and Andrew Arato, *Civil Society and Political Theory*, chap. 8 on "discourse ethics." Cf. the essay by Simone Chambers, "A Critical Theory of Civil Society" in Chambers and Kymlicka, eds., *Alternative Conceptions*, pp. 90–112.

6. The classic version of this argument can be found in A. D. Lindsay, *The Modern Democratic State* (London: Oxford University Press, 1943), chap. 10. Lindsay, however, is more ready than some later theorists to recognize the intrinsic as well as instrumental value of associational life (especially of the "small religious society," in which, he says, democracy began).

7. See Gabriel A. Almond and Sidney Verba, *The Civic Culture: Political Attitudes and Democracy in Five Nations* (Boston: Little, Brown, 1963)—the pioneering study, much imitated and mostly confirmed in the years since its publication.

8. On the positive value of conflict, see Lewis A. Coser, *The Functions of Social Conflict* (Glencoe, Ill.: Free Press, 1956).

9. This point is usefully made in Simone Chambers and Jeffrey Kopstein, "Bad Civil Society," *Political Theory* 29, no. 6 (December 2001), pp. 837–865.

10. Albert O. Hirschman, *Exit, Voice, and Loyalty: Responses to Decline in Firms, Organizations, and States* (Cambridge, Mass.: Harvard University Press, 1970).

11. A. S. P. Woodhouse, ed., *Puritanism and Liberty* (London: J. M. Dent and Sons, 1938), part I: "The Putney Debates," p. 34. I discuss this exchange

in *Obligations: Essays on Disobedience, War, and Citizenship* (Cambridge, Mass.: Harvard University Press, 1970), pp. 196–197.

12. On liberal neutrality vis-à-vis civil society, see Lomasky, "Classical Liberalism and Civil Society," pp. 54–58.

13. See, for example, the books and articles of Susan Moller Okin and Stephen Macedo already cited.

14. I have found little recognition of this rule in the civil society literature. It is not dealt with, for example, in Jean L. Cohen and Andrew Arato, *Civil Society;* Adam Seligman, *The Idea of Civil Society;* or John Keane, *Democracy and Civil Society* (London: Verso, 1988). Feminist writers are more likely to understand the rule. See, for example, Carole Pateman, "The Fraternal Social Contract," in John Keane, ed., *Civil Society and the State* (London: Verso, 1988), pp. 101–127; and Anne Phillips, "Does Feminism Need a Conception of Civil Society?"

15. See Charles Taylor, *Multiculturalism and "The Politics of Recognition,"* ed. Amy Gutmann (Princeton: Princeton University Press, 1992).

16. "Call me mister!" was originally a response to the use of "boy" in addressing black men; it obviously has feminist versions, perhaps not so succinct.

17. This view is classically defended in Loren Lomasky, "Classical Liberalism and Civil Society."

18. For an account of the uses of tax money by religious organizations, see Dean M. Kelley, *Public Funding of Social Services Related to Religious Bodies* (New York: Institute of Human Relations, American Jewish Committee Task Force on Sectarian Social Services and Public Funding, 1990).

19. David Carroll Cochran provides further suggestions along these lines in *The Color of Freedom: Race and Contemporary American Liberalism* (Albany: State University of New York Press, 1999), pp. 141–169.

20. See John Rawls, *Political Liberalism* (New York: Columbia University Press, 1993), pp. 36–37, where Rawls distinguishes pluralism from "reasonable pluralism." I am more interested here in the unqualified "variety of doctrines and views."

21. On the conflicts between individual autonomy and group rights, see Will Kymlicka, "The Good, the Bad, and the Intolerable: Minority Group Rights," *Dissent* (Summer 1996). For the best extended treatment of these issues, and an argument somewhat different from that suggested below, see Will Kymlicka, *Multicultural Citizenship: A Liberal Theory of Minority Rights* (Oxford: Oxford University Press, 1995).

22. See my essay "Pluralism and Social Democracy," *Dissent* (Winter 1998): 47–53.

23. George Konrad, *Antipolitics: An Essay,* trans. Richard E. Allen (New York: Harcourt Brace Jovanovich, 1984).

CHAPTER FIVE. *Deliberation . . . and What Else?*

1. Jürgen Habermas's communication theory has been the subject of a vast critical literature, most of it focused on its technical philosophical aspects. American writers, who mostly avoid technical argument, have so far received less criticism. But see Lynn Sanders, "Against Deliberation," *Political Theory* 25, no. 3 (June 1997): 347–376; and my own "Critique of Philosophical Conversation," aimed only in part at Habermas: *Philosophical Forum* 21 (Fall–Winter, 1989–1990): 182–196.

2. Amy Gutmann and Dennis Thompson, *Democracy and Disagreement* (Cambridge, Mass.: Harvard University Press, 1996); Henry S. Richardson, *Democratic Autonomy: Public Reasoning About the Ends of Policy* (New York: Oxford University Press, 2002).

3. See the interesting discussion of bargaining in Jürgen Habermas, *Between Facts and Norms: Contributions to a Discourse Theory of Law and Democracy*, trans. William Rehg (Cambridge: Polity Press, 1996), pp. 165–167, which ends with a program for the ethical regulation of the bargaining process to bring it as close as possible to deliberation and to avoid outcomes determined by tests of strength; see also chaps. 7 and 8 passim. For an American version of the argument, see Richardson on "deep compromise," in *Democratic Autonomy*, chap. 11.

4. Gutmann and Thompson, *Democracy and Disagreement*, pp. 69–73.

5. See John Rawls's description of the Supreme Court as the "institutional exemplar" of public reason, which radically separates deliberation from politics as we know it: *Political Liberalism* (New York: Columbia University Press, 1993), p. 235.

6. Karl Marx and Friedrich Engels, *The German Ideology*, ed. R. Pascal (New York: International Publishers, 1947), p. 39.

7. Joseph M. Schwartz, *The Permanence of the Political: A Democratic Critique of the Radical Impulse to Transcend Politics* (Princeton: Princeton University Press, 1995).

8. Most importantly, James Fishkin, *Democracy and Deliberation: New Directions for Democratic Reform* (New Haven: Yale University Press, 1991).

9. If the purpose of the juries is simply to add their own conclusions to the mix of ideas and proposals already being debated in the political arena, then they are useful in the same way that think tanks and presidential commissions are useful. If any sort of democratic authority is claimed for them, if the sample replaces the people sampled, they are dangerous.

CHAPTER SIX. *Politics and Passion*

1. *Selected Poems of William Butler Yeats*, ed. M. L. Rosenthal (New York: Macmillan, 1962), pp. 91–92.

2. The translation appears in William Butler Yeats, *Ausgewahlte Werke* (Zurich: Coron-Verlag, 1971), p. 135. I owe this reference to Martina Kessel.

3. Yvor Winters, *Forms of Discovery: Critical and Historical Essays on the Forms of the Short Poem in English* (n.p.: Alan Swallow, 1967), pp. 213–214.

4. The critique of enthusiasm (also religious zeal, fanaticism, and so on) is pervasive in David Hume, *History of England,* roughly from chapter 50 forward. See the analysis in David Miller, *Philosophy and Ideology in Hume's Political Thought* (Oxford: Clarendon Press, 1981), pp. 57, 103, 116–117, 151.

5. John Donne, *Complete Poetry and Selected Prose of John Donne* (New York: Modern Library, 1941), pp. 171, 172. "An Anatomie of the World: The First Anniversary" dates to 1611.

6. Friedrich Engels, *Anti-Duhring* [in English] (Chicago: Charles Kerr, 1935), p. 292.

7. Ralph Waldo Emerson, "Circles," in *Essays: First Series,* in Emerson, *The Complete Essays and Other Writings,* ed. Brooks Atkinson (New York: Modern Library, 1940), p. 290.

8. Albert O. Hirschman, *The Passions and the Interests: Political Arguments for Capitalism Before Its Triumph* (Princeton: Princeton University Press, 1977); Joseph A. Schumpeter, *Imperialism and Social Classes* (New York: Kelley, 1951).

9. For Plato's argument, see *The Republic* II.375.

10. Niccolò Machiavelli, *"The Prince" and "The Discourses,"* trans. Christian E. Detmold (New York: Modern Library, 1940), pp. 121–122.

11. Hirschman, *The Passions and the Interests,* pp. 57–59. The quotation is from James Boswell, *Boswell's Life of Johnson* (New York: Oxford University Press, 1933), vol. 1, p. 567.

12. David Hume, along with other eighteenth-century writers, recognizes and approves of another passion, "benevolence toward strangers," but this is "too weak," he argues, "to counterbalance the love of gain." The latter passion can be directed; it can't be replaced; it drives economic and political life. See Hume, *Moral and Political Philosophy,* ed. Henry D. Aiken (New York: Hafner, 1948), p. 61.

13. See Alexis de Tocqueville, *Democracy in America,* ed. J. P. Mayer and Max Lerner, trans. George Lawrence (New York: Harper and Row, 1966), vol. 2, part II, pp. 497–501.

14. See Jon Elster, *Making Sense of Marx* (Cambridge: Cambridge University Press, 1985), for an argument that stresses that aspect of Marxism.

15. For a representative example, see Bogdan Denitch, *Ethnic Nationalism: The Tragic Death of Yugoslavia,* rev. ed. (Minneapolis: University of Minnesota Press, 1996).

16. See Iris Marion Young's essay "Social Difference as a Political Re-

source," in *Inclusion and Democracy* (Oxford: Oxford University Press, 2000), chap. 3, esp. pp. 109–110.

17. See Diane Rothbard Margolis, *The Fabric of Self: A Theory of Ethics and Emotions* (New Haven: Yale University Press, 1998), chap. 5, for an account of how emotions of attachment and repulsion figure in what she calls the "obligated self" and the "civic self."

18. Ignazio Silone, *Emergency Exit* (New York: Harper and Row, 1968), chap. 7 (trans. Harvey Fergusson).

Conclusion

1. The pioneering book is Charles R. Beitz, *Political Theory and International Relations* (Princeton: Princeton University Press, 1979). More recent works include Thomas Pogge, *Realizing Rawls* (Ithaca, N.Y.: Cornell University Press, 1989); Darrel Moellendorf, *Cosmopolitan Justice* (Boulder, Colo.: Westview Press, 2002); Ian Shapiro and Lea Brilmayer, eds., *Global Justice (Nomos XLI)* (New York: New York University Press, 1999); and Thomas Pogge, ed., *Global Justice* (Oxford: Blackwell, 2001). John Rawls's *The Law of Peoples* (Cambridge, Mass.: Harvard University Press, 1999) is an effort to deny, or at least to qualify, the applicability of his own liberal theory to international society.

2. For an early and insightful study of international civil society, see Paul Wapner, *Environmental Activism and World Civic Politics* (Albany: State University of New York Press, 1996); for a more recent study see John Keane, *Global Civil Society?* (Cambridge: Cambridge University Press, 2003).

3. For a strong critique of state sovereignty, see Brian Barry, "Statism and Nationalism: A Cosmopolitan Critique," in Shapiro and Brilmayer, eds., *Global Justice,* pp. 12–66. For a defense, to which I am indebted, see Neil A. Englehart, "In Defense of State Building: States, Rights, and Justice," *Dissent* (Fall 2003): 18–22.

4. The phrase comes from John Rawls, *A Theory of Justice* (Cambridge, Mass.: Harvard University Press, 1971), p. 72.

5. Iris Marion Young provides a usefully expansive account of the "regulatory regimes" necessary to a decent international society in *Inclusion and Democracy,* chap. 7, esp. pp. 267–268.

6. For a description of how global redistribution might work, see Thomas Pogge, "Priorities of Global Justice," in Pogge, ed., *Global Justice* (Oxford: Blackwell, 2001), pp. 6–23.

7. John Rawls's heroic effort to include what he calls "decent hierarchical societies" in a liberal account of international society, for which he has been much criticized, suggests the problem. See Rawls's *The Law of Peoples,* pp. 64–

70; and the critique by Andrew Kuper, "Rawlsian Global Justice: Beyond *The Law of Peoples* to a Cosmopolitan Law of Persons," *Political Theory* 29, no. 5 (October 2000): 640–674.

APPENDIX: *The Communitarian Critique of Liberalism*

1. Karl Marx, "On the Jewish Question," in *Early Writings*, ed. T. B. Bottomore (London: C. A. Watts, 1963), p. 26.

2. Alasdair MacIntyre, *After Virtue* (Notre Dame, Ind.: University of Notre Dame Press, 1981).

3. Thomas Hobbes, *The Elements of Law*, part I, chap. 9, para. 21. I have noticed that the two favorite writers of communitarian critics of this first kind are Hobbes and Jean-Paul Sartre. Is it possible that the essence of liberalism is best revealed by these two, who were not, in the usual sense of the term, liberals at all?

4. See Albert O. Hirschman's *Exit, Voice, and Loyalty* (Cambridge, Mass.: Harvard University Press, 1970).

5. MacIntyre, *After Virtue*, chaps. 2 and 17.

6. This is Richard Rorty's summary of Michael Sandel's argument: Rorty, "The Priority of Democracy to Philosophy," in Merrill D. Peterson and Robert C. Vaughan, eds., *The Virginia Statute for Religious Freedom* (Cambridge: Cambridge University Press, 1982).

7. Thomas Hobbes, *De Cive*, ed. by Howard Warrender (Oxford: Oxford University Press, 1983), part I, chap. 1.

8. Robert Bellah et al., *Habits of the Heart* (Berkeley: University of California Press, 1985), pp. 21, 290; see Richard Rorty's comment in "Priority," p. 275 n. 12.

9. And also its practical working out, in the career open to talents, the right of free movement, legal divorce, and so on.

10. See A. Campbell et al., *The American Voter* (New York: Wiley, 1960), pp. 147–148.

11. See the evocation of Martin Luther King, Jr., in Bellah et al., *Habits of the Heart*, pp. 249, 252.

12. Roberto Mangabeira Unger, *The Critical Legal Studies Movement* (Cambridge, Mass.: Harvard University Press, 1986), p. 41.

13. Cf. Buff-Coat (Robert Everard) in the Putney debates: "Whatsoever . . . obligations I should be bound unto, if afterwards God should reveal himself, I would break it speedily, if it were a hundred a day." In A. S. P. Woodhouse, ed., *Puritanism and Liberty* (London: J. M. Dent and Sons, 1938), p. 34. Is Buff-Coat the first superliberal or Unger a latter-day Puritan saint?

14. I do not intend a determinist argument here. We mostly move around

within inherited worlds because we find such worlds comfortable and even life-enhancing; but we also move out when we find them cramped—and liberalism makes the escape much easier than it was in preliberal societies.

15. I describe how free-ridership works in ethnic groups in "Pluralism: A Political Perspective," in the *Harvard Encyclopedia of American Ethnic Groups,* ed. Stephan Thernstrom (Cambridge, Mass.: Harvard University Press, 1980), pp. 781–787.

16. John Rawls, *A Theory of Justice* (Cambridge, Mass.: Harvard University Press, 1971), pp. 527ff.

17. See the argument for a modest "perfectionism" (rather than neutrality) in Joseph Raz, *The Morality of Freedom* (Oxford: Clarendon Press, 1986), chaps. 5 and 6.

18. Irving Bernstein, *Turbulent Years: A History of the American Worker, 1933–1941* (Boston: Houghton Mifflin, 1970), chap. 7.

19. See my essay "Socializing the Welfare State," in Amy Gutmann, *Democracy and the Welfare State* (Princeton: Princeton University Press, 1988), pp. 13–26.

20. John Dewey, *The Public and Its Problems* (Athens, Ohio: Swallow Press, 1985), pp. 71–72.

21. This kind of pluralist republicanism is also likely to advance the prospects of what I called "complex equality" in *Spheres of Justice* (New York: Basic Books, 1983). I cannot pursue this question here, but it is worth noting that both liberalism and communitarianism can take egalitarian, nonegalitarian, or antiegalitarian forms. Similarly, the communitarian correction of liberalism can strengthen the old inequalities of traditionalist ways of life, or it can counteract the new inequalities of the liberal market and the bureaucratic state. The "republic of republics" is likely, though by no means certain, to have effects of the second sort.

22. The issue is starkly posed in Michael Sandel, *Liberalism and the Limits of Justice* (Cambridge: Cambridge University Press, 1982); much of the recent discussion is a commentary on or argument with Sandel's book.

23. See Will Kymlicka, "Liberalism and Communitarianism," *Canadian Journal of Philosophy* (June 1988): 181–204.

24. Horace Kallen, *Culture and Democracy in the United States* (New York: Boni and Liveright, 1924).

Index

A

Aboriginal tribes, 50
Abraham, 4–5, 168*n*7
Aggression, military, 126–127
Agitprop, 92–94, 107
Algeria, 30–32
Almond, Gabriel A., 172*n*7
American Civil Liberties Union, 133
Amish, 62, 86
Amnesty International, 133
Anti-Defamation League, 67
Antipolitics, 88, 118, 122
Arabs, 30–32, 48
Arato, Andrew, 172*n*2, 172*n*5, 173*n*14
Aristocracy, 113, 121–122, 124, 127
Aristotle, 102
Association: core-periphery model of, 38; disengagement from, 10–11; forms of, 5–8. *See also* Civil society; Groups; Involuntary association; Voluntary association

Autonomy, x, 1–2, 11–12, 57, 59, 66, 86–87, 173*n*21

B

Bachrach, Peter, 169*n*4
Banting, Keith, 167*n*3
Baptists, 38, 83
Baratz, Morton C., 169*n*4
Bargaining, 96–97, 104, 108, 174*n*3
Beitz, Charles R., 176*n*1
Berman, Sheri, 172*n*4
Birnbaum, Pierre, 170*n*10
Black Americans, 38–39, 41, 58, 83
Bourne, Randolph, 163
Bribery, 25, 100–101
Bunyan, John, 4–5, 168*n*7
Bush, George H. W., 82